Jacobo Schifter, PhD

Macho Love
Sex Behind Bars
in Central America

Pre-publication
REVIEWS,
COMMENTARIES,
EVALUATIONS . . .

"**T**his is a powerful book about men in jails, their sexuality, and AIDS prevention, but most of all about the vicissitudes of love, hope, and redemption."

Sara Sharratt, PhD
Professor Emeritus of Counseling,
Sonoma State University,
Robnert Park, CA

"**M**acho Love: Sex Behind Bars in Central America provides a fascinating account of male sexual culture in Central American prisons. This well-written English translation of Jacobo Schifter's book challenges facile explanations of male sexuality

in terms of rigid categories. Many readers will find some of their most basic assumptions about human sexuality called into question by the men's stories.

The prisoners' narratives are effectively used to complement the author's analysis of prison sexuality, an analysis that is always mindful of the social context in which the inmates live.

Macho Love is an important book and a valuable contribution to the research literature on sexuality."

Gregory M. Herek, PhD
Research Psychologist,
University of California,
Davis, CA

Macho Love
Sex Behind Bars in Central America

HAWORTH Gay & Lesbian Studies

John P. De Cecco, PhD
Editor in Chief

Our Families, Our Values: Snapshots of Queer Kinship edited by Robert E. Goss and Amy Adams Squire Strongheart

Gay/Lesbian/Bisexual/Transgender Public Policy Issues: A Citizen's and Administrator's Guide to the New Cultural Struggle edited by Wallace Swan

Rough News, Daring Views: 1950s' Pioneer Gay Press Journalism by Jim Kepner

Family Secrets: Gay Sons—A Mother's Story by Jean M. Baker

Twenty Million New Customers: Understanding Gay Men's Consumer Behavior by Steven M. Kates

The Empress Is a Man: Stories from the Life of José Sarria by Michael R. Gorman

Acts of Disclosure: The Coming-Out Process of Contemporary Gay Men by Marc E. Vargo

Queer Kids: The Challenges and Promise for Lesbian, Gay, and Bisexual Youth by Robert E. Owens

Looking Queer: Body Image and Identity in Lesbian, Gay, Bisexual, and Transgender Communities edited by Dawn Atkins

Love and Anger: Essays on AIDS, Activism, and Politics by Peter F. Cohen

Dry Bones Breathe: Gay Men Creating Post-AIDS Identities and Cultures by Eric Rofes

Lila's House: Male Prostitution in Latin America by Jacobo Schifter

A Consumer's Guide to Male Hustlers by Joseph Itiel

Trailblazers: Profiles of America's Gay and Lesbian Elected Officials by Kenneth E. Yeager

Rarely Pure and Never Simple: Selected Essays by Scott O'Hara

Navigating Differences: Friendships Between Gay and Straight Men by Jammie Price

In the Pink: The Making of Successful Gay- and Lesbian-Owned Businesses by Sue Levin

Behold the Man: The Hype and Selling of Male Beauty in Media and Culture by Edisol Wayne Dotson

Untold Millions: Secret Truths About Marketing to Gay and Lesbian Consumers by Grant Lukenbill

It's a Queer World: Deviant Adventures in Pop Culture by Mark Simpson

In Your Face: Stories from the Lives of Queer Youth by Mary L. Gray

Military Trade by Steven Zeeland

Longtime Companions: Autobiographies of Gay Male Fidelity by Alfred Lees and Ronald Nelson

From Toads to Queens: Transvestism in a Latin American Setting by Jacobo Schifter

The Construction of Attitudes Toward Lesbians and Gay Men edited by Lynn Pardie and Tracy Luchetta

Lesbian Epiphanies: Women Coming Out in Later Life by Karol L. Jensen

Smearing the Queer: Medical Bias in the Health Care of Gay Men by Michael Scarce

Macho Love: Sex Behind Bars in Central America by Jacobo Schifter

When It's Time to Leave Your Lover: A Guide for Gay Men by Neil Kaminsky

Strategic Sex: Why They Won't Keep It in the Bedroom by D. Travers Scott

One of the Boys: Masculinity, Homophobia, and Modern Manhood by David Plummer

Homosexual Rites of Passage: A Road to Visibility and Validation by Marie Mohler

Male Lust: Power, Pleasure, and Transformation by Kerwin Kay, Jill Nagle, and Baruch Gould

Macho Love
Sex Behind Bars
in Central America

Jacobo Schifter, PhD

The Haworth Hispanic/Latino Press
An Imprint of The Haworth Press, Inc.
New York • London • Oxford

Published by

The Haworth Hispanic/Latino Press, an imprint of The Haworth Press, Inc., 10 Alice Street, Binghamton, NY 13904-1580

English translation by Christina E. Feeny.

Cover design by Jennifer M. Gaska.

Library of Congress Cataloging-in-Publication Data

Schifter, Jacobo.
    [Amor de machos. English]
    Macho love : sex behind bars in Central America / Jacobo Schifter.
       p.   cm.
    Includes bibliographical references and index.
    ISBN 1-56023-965-4 (hc. : alk. paper)—ISBN 1-56023-966-2 (pbk. : alk. paper)
    1. Prisoners—Central America—Sexual behavior. 2. Prisoners—Health and hygiene—Central America. 3. Homosexuality—Central America. I. Title.
HV8836.S3513 1999
365'6—dc21
                                                99-28342
                                                   CIP

For Ellyn Kaschak, my friend and sister. Blood relationships are not necessarily the closest or those vested with the greatest solidarity. We have both learned that families have not been the best creation in history and that to make them work, it is necessary to build them, like sexuality. To maintain a relationship of more than thirty years, you need something more than shared genes or surnames. As a writer and professor at the University of California, Ellyn is well-known. But to me she has been a great influence for having taught me about the marvels of cynical Jewish humor and the leftist, questioning, revolutionary vein of my people. Although she may not appreciate my obsession with Jews such as Levinas and Derrida (as males with somewhat unclear attitudes toward feminism), we share the idea that Judaism means something more than following religious precepts: it is a preoccupation with how we might make this a more just world and respect the difference, the "Other" of Levinas.

ABOUT THE AUTHOR

Jacobo Schifter, PhD, is the Regional Director of ILPES (the Latin American Health and Prevention Institute), an AIDS prevention program financed by the Netherlands' government. One of the most prolific writers in Latin America, Dr. Schifter wrote books on the Costa Rican civil war, U.S.-Costa Rican relations, and Costa Rican anti-Semitism before shifting his interests when AIDS started to affect the Central American region. He then established the first regional institute to fight the epidemic and created dozens of inno- vative programs, such as AIDS hotlines and AIDS prevention workshops for Latin gays, prisoners, street children, Indians, male sex workers, and other minority groups. Dr. Schifter also started to publish controversial books on AIDS, including *The Formation of a Counterculture: AIDS and Homosexuality in Costa Rica* (1989), *Men Who Love Men* (1992), *Eyes That Do Not See: Psychiatry and Homophobia* (1997), *Lila's House* (1998), and *From Toads to Queens* (Haworth, 1999). These books have become best-sellers in the region and have also played a part in changing many Latin governments' discriminatory policies against people with AIDS.

CONTENTS

Preface   ix

Acknowledgments   xi

Chapter 1. Background: The Study and the Prisons   1

Information Sources   1
Admission   3
First Impact   7
The Scale of the Homosexual Phenomenon   11
Two Views of Homosexuality   13

Chapter 2. The *Cachero* and the Transvestite   17

Initiation   19
Sexual Practices   29
Cachero Love   33

Chapter 3. The *Cachero* and the Kid   35

Initiation   45
The *Güila's* Story   47
Changes in Sexual Practices   51

Chapter 4. Foxes   53

The Revolutionary Backside   57
Power and Sex   58

Chapter 5. Relationships of Power and Money   65

Prostitution Among Foxes   71
Rape   73

Chapter 6. Risk Factors in Sexual Relationships   81

Alcoholism and Drug Addiction   81
Condom Use and Attitudes Toward Condoms   83
Intimacy   84

Chapter 7. Suggestions for Prevention   **89**

Drawbacks   92
The Holistic Model   93
Sexual Education   97
Accepting the Lesser Evil   98
Recognition of Homosexual Couples   98
Assistance in Detoxification   99
Prevention of Violence   100
Playing with Free Time   100
Microenterprises   101

Epilogue   **103**

Notes   **107**

Index   **111**

Preface

This study represents more than ten years of research in Costa Rican and Central American prisons. My interest in writing about homosexuality in these institutions stems from my commitment to fight against HIV infection. Back in 1988, I began giving AIDS-prevention workshops as part of my work with the former Asociación de Lucha Contra el Sida, today known as the Latin American Institute for Prevention and Health Education (ILPES). As a result of these efforts, I was contracted by the World Health Organization (WHO) to conduct a study about the knowledge and practices of men who have sex with other men in Costa Rica. This study would include a section on the situation in the penitentiary system. Some of the data gathered from that study has been used in this book. Later, I began a series of workshops with prison inmates to increase their knowledge about AIDS and improve prevention efforts. The different histories of hundreds of prisoners were imprinted forever in my mind.

The objective of this book is to reveal part of the sexual culture of prisons in order to improve AIDS-prevention programs. The aim is to study the types of relationships that occur in these institutions and the factors that place inmates at risk of contracting the HIV virus. This data has been facilitated thanks to a series of studies carried out with the close collaboration of ILPES and the Ministry of Justice. Finally, I would like to make some general recommendations so that the holistic approach to prevention may take new leaps forward in the fight against AIDS.

I believe that all attempts to "colonize" the sexual culture of prison inmates—whether through medical lectures, psychoanalytical therapies, mandatory AIDS testing, scientific pamphlets in condom packets, theater plays that spread terror of AIDS, or visits by social workers from the Department for the Control of AIDS—will fail unless they learn to respect that culture. This type of sensitivity has been demonstrated in Costa Rica by the Ministry of Justice and the Department of Social Adaptation. I hope that many other justice ministries across the continent will be interested in examining this policy, both its many successes and its failures.

Another wish, no less important to me, is to describe how a sexual culture far removed from the discourse of Costa Rica's middle classes is built up by the most dispossessed sectors of our society. This prison culture develops parallel to the predominant culture and, at the same time, allows us to look in a different way at our own culture. Even within a sexual counterculture, relations of power are established that create resistance. Any discourse or practice that attempts to set general rules for the entire population has its saboteurs, its revolutionaries, and its martyrs.

Acknowledgments

I would like to acknowledge the collaboration of my colleagues at ILPES, Antonio Bustamante, Lidia Montero, Julián González, Johnny Madrigal, and Dino Starcevic, who helped me review this book. Héctor Elizondo, as always, was my main critic. I would also like to thank my colleagues at the Department of Social Adaptation and the Ministry of Justice of Costa Rica, who have collaborated both with ILPES and with me personally. I consider this ministry a pioneer in recognizing the problems encountered in prisons and not trying to hide them as others have done. Although the situations mentioned in this book are common to all penitentiaries around the world, very few authorities are willing to acknowledge them.

However, the events described in this book are the exclusive responsibility of the author and do not represent the position of ILPES or the Ministry of Justice.

Chapter 1

Background:
The Study and the Prisons

INFORMATION SOURCES

This study consists of several research phases. The first phase was conducted in 1989, as part of a program financed by the World Health Organization, in which nine countries participated.[1] The objective was to study the risk of HIV infection among men who have sex with other men. To this end, a questionnaire known as the Homosexual Response Survey, prepared jointly by all nine countries, was used. To assess the possibility of circulating the questionnaire, in-depth interviews were conducted with eight openly homosexual or transvestite inmates in one prison. As a result, twenty-two out of the twenty-four inmates who were registered as homosexuals in the prison files agreed to complete the questionnaire. Only two were unwilling to participate. Thus, the sample obtained represents the group of "obvious" homosexuals or transvestites, as they describe themselves.

To strengthen our research in this particular prison, an additional questionnaire was circulated among the prison's administrative staff. In January 1990, staff were asked to complete a short, self-administered questionnaire, with questions relating to symptoms, origins, and forms of prevention of HIV virus as well as attitudes toward homosexuals. Data were gathered from thirty-seven prison officials.

The second phase of this research program began in 1991, when ILPES launched its AIDS-prevention workshops for Costa Rican prison inmates. The courses were open to all prisoners and, by 1997, more than 1,000 had signed up for them. These workshops have enabled us to discuss issues relating to the sexual culture in prisons. Since each course consists of eight three-hour sessions, and covers a wide range of topics related to sexuality, drugs, love, violence, AIDS prevention, and other subjects, the workshops have provided a very rich source of information about sexual activity in prison. In 1993, we studied the pretest and posttest responses of a total of 188 inmates of all sexual orientations. However, many participants preferred not to discuss very intimate details in public. Therefore, to gain further information on specific topics, in January and February 1995, we conducted in-depth interviews with a dozen inmates known as *cacheros* (men who perform active anal sex), *zorras* (in-the-closet homosexuals), and *güilas* (young gay men), the categories not included in the first phase of the study. Workshop participants also recommended friends who fit into these three categories, and most participated willingly in the interviews. Some had participated in the courses and others had not. The interviews lasted between one and one and a half hours each. All participants were interviewed for two or three sessions. The average duration of the entire interview was three hours.

The interviewers were gay men who have worked for several years with support programs for prison inmates run by nongovernmental organizations. They have gained inmates' trust and much of the information obtained proves this fact. In the course of the interviews, prisoners discuss drug trafficking, prostitution, and even homicides that have occurred within prison walls. Without our assurances of complete confidentiality, they would not have revealed much of this information. The fact that the interviewers displayed familiarity with sexual jargon and culture succeeded, on many occasions, in eliciting admissions of certain unrecognized practices and feelings on the part of interviewees.

With the introduction of the holistic workshops for inmates, certain things changed in the sexual culture of prisons. The results of evaluations show that sexual communication improved, condom use increased, knowledge about AIDS improved, and homophobia decreased.[2] Nevertheless, these changes have not altered the main sexual relationships that predominate in the different prisons, and therefore the data gathered during the three phases of the study is still valid.

To protect the privacy of the inmates and prison staff who participated in the studies, we have changed their names or used pseudonyms. We have also omitted the names of the prisons selected for the sample, together with any descriptions that might identify the penitentiaries and their inmates.

ADMISSION

San Sebastián is San José's admission prison, from which prisoners are sent to other penal institutions. This facility has a long name, typical of official jargon: the Center for Institutional Attention of San José. But to the public it is known simply as San Sebastián, the name of the district in which it is located, a marginal area to the south of San José, just a few minutes from anywhere, like so many places in the Costa Rican capital.

The building is austere. New arrivals are greeted by the somber, pale green walls of the main facade, and by a sculpture of a group of seated peasants who appear to gaze coldly and lifelessly. At night, they often frighten passersby who do not realize that they are made of stone. "Why are there statues of peasants in front of a prison where most of the inmates are from the city?" a foreign visitor asked us one day. "So people will understand that the lack of land and the influx of peasants into the cities is what has screwed up this country," we replied, without believing our own explanation.

Beyond the prison's outer fence is the reception counter where a female official inquires about the purpose of our visit. We then face the hostile or indifferent expressions of the guards who open the glass door that leads to the prison's administrative area.

This is the prison's "official" face, the one seen by occasional visitors and staff. There is another reality that can be sensed from the building itself, if you walk a little farther toward the south. Here, things change radically.

The walls suddenly lose their color, and become gray and stained with damp. This is where visitors stand in line—a line that sometimes seems interminable—waiting to visit the inmates. There are men, of course, but the majority are women, presumably mothers, wives, or girlfriends. They go through the admission procedure on visiting days: the long wait while documents are checked, the inquisitive looks of the guards, a more or less thorough search. Above, on top of the prison walls, are the guard posts, the barbed wire, and the weapons.

But there is yet another reality, the harshest of all: the reality of the inmates, the prison's permanent residents. They arrive here under escort, guarded inside the *perreras* or dog cages (as the official prison transport vehicles are popularly termed) and are driven through an enormous gray metal gate.

New arrivals are usually handcuffed and suddenly pass from the pitch darkness of the prison van into the blinding light outside. They are quickly taken to the reception area, where they undergo administrative procedures for their admission to prison. Seated on a long wooden bench, under the watchful gaze of blue-uniformed guards, new arrivals wait their turn to be admitted. Most are poorly dressed, dirty individuals, who sit in silence and look apprehensively at everything around them.

Sitting at an old typewriter, one of the guards fills in the registration forms, and then takes the prisoners' fingerprints. Afterward, they are taken to an office where, after an interview, they are assigned to a particular section of the prison and their treatment program is defined. We hear a new inmate being interviewed. "Profession?" asks the prison official. "Bank manager," replies the prisoner.

Inmates who are here for the first time and have not yet been sentenced are sent to Section A, the remand section. The same fate awaits first-timers who are admitted after sentencing. Section B1 is where reoffending prisoners who have already been sentenced are placed. Any inmate who has problems with another resident of B1 is sent to Section C1.

Repeat offenders are sent to Sections B2 or C2. Other Costa Rican prisons have maximum security wings that house violent inmates, those serving very long sentences, or prisoners who must be isolated for personal security reasons.

Once the admission procedure is completed, the new arrival begins his journey toward the heart of the jail. He moves along narrow passageways painted blue and cream, through a succession of metal gates and electric locks, which are operated by invisible hands. As he goes deeper into the jail, the faces become increasingly hostile.

Suddenly, reality hits him: when he passes through the last gate of the administrative section, he comes face-to-face with his new world, the interior of the prison. The officer who guards this point performs a final search and a second metal gate opens. This is the boundary between freedom and captivity. It is where the prison reveals its true face.

Here, my guide and contact, Pico de Lora ("Parrot Beak") is waiting to introduce me to prison society. I see him walk toward me. He is about thirty years old and quite attractive looking, with fine features. His hair is black with a few gray hairs. He is shirtless and has a phenomenal chest, like a bodybuilder. "Good afternoon," he says in a thick voice. "Are you the one who's going to write about us?" he asks. "Yes, I want to write a book about sexual culture and you were recommended to help make the contacts for me," I reply confidently. "Well, are you going to write about sex or culture?" "No, Pico de Lora, you don't understand. Sexual culture is one subject," I answer obligingly. "You're the one who doesn't understand shit," he retorts. "Are you really going to write a book or have you come as a voyeur, so you can jerk off at home later?" he asks in all seriousness. "I'm here to write a book, and if I jerk off later that's not your problem," I answer, to win his respect. Pico de Lora grins and asks no more questions.

Behind bars, a makeshift *pulpería* (corner store) sells refreshments, sweets, and packaged snacks to the inmates. "This is the International Mall, says the store manager, another inmate. "We take all credit cards here except Holdup Express. Problem is, we don't give any of 'em back." "And what do you sell here?" I ask. "Well, anything from a goddamn pizza to duck à l'orange. Weekends we have spiced foxes," answers the store manager. Pico de Lora winks and says, "The store manager is the fox."

Beyond are some large metal containers filled with garbage and flies, where the waste from the cell blocks is collected. "The fly is the national bird of San Seba," says my companion. "Some guys even keep them as pets." This is the beginning of the long passageway, lined with wire mesh, which leads to the prisoners' final destination. The sense of smell is the first casualty here; it is impossible to escape from the penetrating odor of Carbolina, a strong disinfectant used to keep cockroaches and other pests at bay. This substance is mixed with water and sprayed everywhere. "If you don't like the smell, I'll spray you with Paco Rabanne in a moment," says Pico de Lora.

It is also impossible to escape the stares, which visitors are warned not to return. New arrivals must endure the gaze of dozens of pairs of eyes, from every direction: from those wandering along the passageway, from the dark windows of the modules, which are separated from them by a small garden area. "Why do the inmates stare?" we ask Pico de Lora. "Well, the eyes are like a color TV. When you come into jail, the guys see different things," he replies. "Different colors?" I ask in surprise. Pico de Lora becomes irritated at these questions and, with some reluctance, explains:

> Yeah, it's like you're watching a black and white movie and you suddenly get it in color. For example, I'm looking at you now in black and white, but I notice you have a gold chain. This appears in pure color because I want it. Each guy sees color in the things he wants. A *cachero* will see your butt all pink, and a mugger will see your wallet red, full of colorful toucans. ["Toucan" is slang for a 5,000 colon note, approximately $20.]

Pico de Lora is right in a way. We all have black and white screens and colors are added according to what our minds decide is of interest; there is no single object shared by everyone, no general interest. The inmates see the new arrival in accordance with their personal desires, and these may vary every moment. I begin to feel aware of my entire body. I feel like a walking rainbow. "What is a *cachero*?" I ask Pico de Lora. "Oh, don't be a jerk!" he replies, not believing my ignorance. As he does not answer I ask, "And why a pink butt?"

I remain perplexed, thinking about televisions, about all of our minds giving color to what we like and leaving in black and white what we do not. It sounds funny, but it conceals a great tragedy. Everyone is into his own thing; only desire matters. We are in the same prison and each person chooses what he sees. There cannot be much impartiality in my eyes. I have my colors too. "Pico de Lora, does this mean that there cannot be one book, but thousands, about this jail?" I ask, not expecting an answer. "What colors are you seeing now?" he asks.

As one moves down the corridor, one is overwhelmed by a feeling of desperation. It is here that, for the first time, one senses freedom ebbing away. At the end of the passageway, dismal bars rise up at the entrance to each module, the inmate's final destination. Crowds of men are crammed into cells that were built to accommodate half their number. "Who designed this?" I ask innocently. "Designed?" Pico de Lora asks in a sarcastic tone. "Excuse me, but design sounds like something fancy and this here is a shit hole. The guy who did this, or conceived it, shall we say, was a butcher or a public architect—it's all the same shit."

We go into a cell. It smells of sweat, but it does not stink. The inmates are clean and they all turn to stare at us. "Is this guy a toad (an informer) or a public official?" they will ask themselves. "Hi guys," I say, "I'm here to write a book." "Well, look here, Truman 'Chayote' just arrived to do a novel!" replies a venomous transvestite. "I'm Mother Teresa and a great whore," continues the transvestite, who introduces herself as Clitoris.* "No, really, I want to write a book about you," I insist, as I ask myself why the hell I'm doing this work. I fix my gaze on Clitoris. I think she is the ugliest queen I have seen in my entire life: she has drooping breasts that have deflated for lack of silicone, a mouth swollen from many beatings, and a nose more twisted than Friday the thirteenth. "Well, girls, since Princess Diana started avoiding journalists, the paparazzi have nothing to do, so they come to photograph us. I'm going to make sure that my chauffeur hears my screams so he can take me immediately," says Clitoris, trying to wisecrack. The rest of the inmates, who are accustomed to her outbursts, laugh with a mixture of sympathy and contempt. "OK, that's enough!" says Pico de Lora. "Let our friend do his interviews so he can tell people what goes on here." "Okay, so what's your book about?" asks Toro. "I'm here to write about sex in jail," I answer with some trepidation. "Holy cow! I'm going to collapse," exclaims Clitoris, pretending to faint.

FIRST IMPACT

Prisons are characterized by overcrowding, the result of a growing population, growing crime, and increased penalties for certain offenses such as drug trafficking. In the prisons we selected to conduct our interviews, overpopulation in 1997 exceeded 100 percent. Facilities built to accommodate 300 inmates now hold more than 1,000. Blocks designed to house 40 people hold an average of 100 prisoners. Cells with capacity for 4 people now have up to 15. In 1997, the prison population in Costa Rica totaled 5,730. Pico de

---

*Throughout this book, transvestites are referred to as "she," which is customary among these men.

Lora tells me that congestion produces violence. "When you put rats in small spaces, they end up eating each other," he says sadly. "Here, the rats have more freedom than we do and they're less stressed out because they can wander up and down," he adds.

Overcrowding means that many inmates do not even have a bed or a mattress to sleep on. The bathrooms are always full, and prisoners must wait for hours to answer the call of nature. In some prisons, water pours into the cells when it rains. Rats and cockroaches can be seen everywhere. "In one place there's a nest of rats that are so big that even Racumín [a rat poison] doesn't kill them," says a transvestite called Enriqueta.[3] Mosquitoes attack incessantly. "Anyone who doesn't have incense to burn has to suffer mosquito bites all night," says Jara. "Only people who eat garlic are saved from being eaten alive."

In many prisons, there is nothing for inmates to do. Opportunities for work or study are very limited. In some, possibilities for work or study were nonexistent until ILPES became involved in 1993. Inmates were locked in their cells all day, except for a brief period when they could go outdoors to get some sun or attend Christian services. The classroom in one prison has only twelve desks. The computer workshop can hold only ten people. However, the prison population varies between 700 and 1,000 inmates. In the country's largest prison, with more than 1,500 inmates, opportunities for study are greater, but only a small percentage of prisoners actually benefit. Work options are also very limited. Very few companies avail themselves of cheap prison labor.

The cells are divided into small niches or dens, which provide the only personal space for inmates. Using a mattress, a blanket, a sheet, or cardboard, prisoners close off the small area of their beds for themselves. These niches are used for many things: to plan a robbery, make a confession, masturbate, have sexual relations, or plan an escape. Although you cannot see inside, everything can be heard, so real privacy is nonexistent. "I'm aware of every fart in every den," says Lola, another transvestite. "Nothing can be hidden here. The only privacy you have is the law of silence, which stops inmates from informing the guards." However, inmates consider that there is privacy when others pretend not to see what goes on. "Here they rape a guy in front of everyone. They go into a den and you hear the screams and the moans," says Carlos. "Nevertheless, they pretend that because of the mattress, nobody saw anything."

Prison is a world of men. Not only is there close physical contact between them, but emotional contact also. "From the time you arrive here, the only company you have is other men. You eat, shit, sleep, and fuck with them," says Pablo. Prison makes men seek other males to talk, to be intimate, to plan and dream together. "You're forced to share everything with them. What you once talked about with your mother, your girlfriend, or your son, you now tell your cellmate," explains Luis.

However, most prisoners arrive completely unprepared for the culture they encounter in jail. José, for example, could not believe that the attractive "girl" he saw passing by his cell was actually a man. "I know I should have realized that this is a men's prison, but I was so shocked, it never crossed my mind that she was a homosexual. I thought she was a female prison officer interviewing an inmate. When I realized, I nearly fainted." Enrique entered a section where a transvestite was passionately kissing her man. It was the first time he had ever seen two men kissing. "I thought they were going to grab me next. Nobody explained to me what was going on." Others, like Carlos, arrive in the middle of a lovers' squabble. "I was all depressed and, when I got to my cell, there was a fight going on between an old guy and a young kid. The first was accusing the second of having given his ass to someone else. The young kid asked me, "It's a lie that I was with Pico, right?" I felt sorry for him, so I said, "Yeah, I never saw you with Pico." In some cases, young men or transvestites are raped on their very first night in prison. Claudia, a transvestite, recalls: "I didn't have time to adapt to anything. That same night I was raped by three sex maniacs."

The system punishes crime with captivity and overcrowding. People find themselves in such close physical proximity that inmates have more contact with each other than they would in any other situation. "Even with my wife I never had the physical contact that I have with my cellmates," says Luis. "I know what they eat, how they sleep, how and when they go to the bathroom, what they think, what they want, and what they desire." Communication is so intense that Pedro believes, "There's no relationship as close as this in other spheres of life. Outside, you don't spend twenty-four hours a day with anyone. It's not usual to get to know someone so intensely."

This physical and emotional proximity leads to increased homosexual relations. "It's a short step to take from relying on a companion for everything to ending up making love with him," reveals José. "Perhaps not everyone does it, perhaps not with your best friend, but the fact is that sooner or later—and generally sooner than you think—you end up falling in love with a man," says Fernando. According to the results of a questionnaire completed by 188 inmates who attended the AIDS-prevention workshops in 1993, only 23 percent believe that homosexual activity in prison is very limited, while 72 percent admit that it exists to some degree.[4]

Captivity produces a kind of stress which, according to Hart, leads to radical changes in sexual behavior. Not only do homosexual relations occur, but inmates' libido increases considerably.[5] Juan Carlos believes that prison has made him more "horny." "Now I need to fuck every day. What I used to do in a week, I now do daily. I feel a great need to screw guys, day and night." Sex is one of the few pleasures to be found in jail. For some, it's "party time" every day, since an orgy can happen in any cell.

Prison culture is more tolerant of homosexuality. Mario tells us that "the first thing you notice in the block is the ease with which men kiss each other and go around holding hands in front of everyone." No one bothers to look at couples who come together at night. "You can hear moans and screams of pleasure inside different dens," he adds. Mario says the rest of the inmates "jerk off listening to the *cacheros* screwing the gays." However masculine one might be, "there's homosexuality all around."

In some prisons, the level of tolerance is so great that "beauty pageants" are held. Transvestites take advantage of weekends to organize these events. "I was Miss Soda 1995," a twenty-three-year-old transvestite, Lola, tells us proudly. The competition, she says, was very tough because there were a lot of contestants. "But I was the most beautiful, to the annoyance of most of those big whores." Lola obtained almost forty votes more than the next runner-up. "The public was fair," she recalls, "because I don't use hormones like La Chepa—she's more artificial than a silicone tit."

Inmates even recognize "married" couples. When a *cachero* gets together with a transvestite, the rest know that the latter is "his woman" and "you better not touch her because you'll get your hand cut off," explains La Castilla, an older transvestite. "All we need is for the Great Traitor (a well-known religious leader who is rumored to be homosexual, even though he persecutes gays) to come here and do a religious wedding," he adds. Couples are so accepted that anniversary parties are sometimes held. La Castilla continued, "One queen even claimed she was pregnant. The truth is, she was constipated." Rosa, another transvestite, recalls, "I was the godmother at a wedding in a prison I don't want to remember. We bought a wedding cake and we dressed the queen in white, with the sheets from three cells. It was an amazingly beautiful dress, because La Chica Oregano, another queen from there, had made a crown from coconut shells and filled them with white garlic. You didn't know if it was Dracula's daughter or a real bride getting married."

In some prisons, inmates found performing sodomy are punished and placed in sections where there is less freedom. However, it is very unusual for the guards to enter the blocks or the cells at night. And if they do, the inmates warn each other. "I was in a kind of embarrassing situation, if you get my meaning. I was having the best of best times, when I heard someone say: "Chepa, get it out . . . there's a raid."

The guards generally prefer to look the other way when they find a couple engaged in sodomy. According to one guard, prison relationships are so intense that when they take a "kid" (a young man) or a transvestite to another block, as punishment for having been caught red-handed, there are men who slash their wrists in desperation. "The pain of separation is such a big problem that it's better to leave them in peace together," he adds. "Well," says a transvestite, "it depends on the guard. Some are as gay as us, and they make eyes at us when they catch us in the act. One said to me, 'Hey, Blondie, finish what you're eating and then come and give me some.' Others are real assholes and send us to the punishment cells on the slightest suspicion."

THE SCALE OF THE HOMOSEXUAL PHENOMENON

The question of how widespread homosexual practice is in prisons is as old as the penitentiary system itself. Havelock Ellis,[6] in his

famous book *Studies in the Psychology of Sex*, says that approximately 80 percent of men are sexually perverse, though he recog-
nizes that in their "desperate moments, I believe all of them really
are." Joseph F. Fishman, in his book which has become a classic,
Sex Practices of Prisoners, published in 1934, believes the rate of
occurrence in North American prisons is between 30 and 40 percent.[7] As a way of preventing homosexuality in prisons, Fishman
recommends allowing conjugal visits. His book turned into a pro-
test at the lack of sexual freedom—understood as heterosexual freedom—in prisons. In Costa Rica, prisoners now have a right to
conjugal visits. However, Fishman's description of homosexual
relations in his study of North American prisons is identical to ours.

According to data gathered during the holistic workshops in 1993,
72 percent of the participants admit that homosexual relations occur in
prison. More than 50 percent agree that the incidence of homosexual
relations is medium to high.[8]

Taking account of the fact that, in addition to couples, there are
older men who seduce young inmates (known as "kids"), in-the-closet
homosexuals, bisexuals who have occasional sexual relations with
in-the-closet homosexuals or with openly gay men, prison staff who
have sexual relations with inmates, male homosexual visitors, and
prisoners who establish homosexual relationships outside the jail when
they are allowed out to work, it is reasonable to assume that more than
70 percent of prisoners engage in homosexual practices. The inmates
themselves confirm this. Luis tells us that of the 700 inmates in his jail
"about 500 do it," and Juan thinks that "forty percent of the guys have
homosexual relations." As we shall see later, one male prostitute has
had relations with 25 percent of the prisoners. According to Toro, in
certain blocks "all the guys sodomize." He adds, "Look, they used to
call the guys in my gang The Lions, because of their reputation for
being butchers. Now they call them The Felines because, though
they're killers, they're a bunch of queers."

It is not surprising that the incidence of venereal disease in La
Reforma, Costa Rica's largest prison, should be high. During a twelve-
month period, 15 percent of the transvestites and homosexuals who
completed the questionnaire contracted syphilis and 8 percent contracted gonorrhea. Infection is frequent among both transvestites and
other inmates.[9]

TWO VIEWS OF HOMOSEXUALITY

It is important to point out that perceptions about homosexuality vary greatly in different communities. Among the middle classes, homosexuality is seen as a psychological condition that supposedly develops in stages. This view is more in line with modern psychology, which postulates theories of normality and abnormality. According to those who take the "modern" view, if a person turns out to be homosexual, it is because there was a deviation in their natural development toward heterosexuality. They tend to blame parents or society for the supposed abnormality. Their aversion to this sexual preference is associated with a homosexual "character," with supposed psychological abnormalities.

Among the lower classes, to which many inmates belong, homosexuality is seen as an inversion of gender that has nothing to do with psychological development. Individuals from the lower classes generally regard sexuality in terms of the body, rather than other factors. Homosexual people are those who exchange the masculine for the feminine. A man can be heterosexual if he is masculine, and vice versa for women. This is why *cacheros* are not perceived as homosexuals.

The Prison Staff

During the in-depth interviews conducted with the prison staff, we asked them to respond to two general questions about homosexuality: its possible origins and their own attitudes toward homosexuals.

The results show that many consider homosexuality to be a disease. None described homosexuality as just another expression of sexuality, or as the characteristic of a sexual or cultural minority.

Prison staff have a concept of homosexuality that we shall call modern. This means that, influenced by psychiatric thinking, they consider that sexuality is determined by the object of desire: people are homosexual, heterosexual, or bisexual according to whom they have sexual relations with. If a man has sex with another man, he is considered homosexual or bisexual, but never heterosexual. Both the active and the passive partner in this relationship are seen as homosexual. In this regard, they differ from the inmates, as we shall see.

The Inmates

Inmates also regard homosexuality as something abnormal, since the homophobic discourse in this country is too strong for them to question it. But despite this attitude, there are major differences between the views of the officers and the inmates. Unlike the prison staff, inmates only regard transvestites as homosexuals. The vast majority believe that homosexuals are "gays," which for them means transvestites. Men who perform sodomy, but who are active and masculine, do not fall into that category, but instead are termed *cacheros*. They are not considered homosexuals in the sexual culture of prisons. "No, no!" says Daniel. "Homosexuals are queers, not machos. I'm supermacho. Can't you see I've got balls? The fact I screw a kid has nothing to do with it. Any man would do the same in my situation." José shares his opinion: "Look, a *cachero* who screws a gay is never considered one. Don't tell me that because I've fucked three assholes at knifepoint that I'm a homosexual, or because I go with La Chepa. Or that some rich kid from San José is more of a man than I am because he's with a broad. Manhood isn't seen that way here," he concludes.

There are several reasons that explain this difference in perceptions between the two groups. In the first place, the inmates generally belong to a lower social class than the prison staff. (It must be borne in mind that of the 188 inmates who attended the AIDS-prevention workshops and who answered the questionnaire, only 7 percent had completed their high school education).[10] Among the lower classes, the modern idea that sexual orientation is determined by the object of sexual attraction is not so widespread. Rather, the predominant idea is that people are divided according to whether they are active or passive. In other words, they believe that *sexual practice* is what determines whether a person is a man or a woman. In popular culture, the man is the penetrator—whether of men, women, children, or animals. Any person who is penetrated is feminine, whether a man, woman, child, or animal. A man who penetrates another man, as happens in prison, continues to be a man.

Unlike the prison staff, the inmates also have a less "environmentalist" vision of the etiology of homosexuality. This means that their perception is more "essentialist"—in other words, they believe that homosexuals are born that way and that little can be done to change them. Very few consider that the influence of others, sexual abuse, or family circumstances are related to homosexuality. Luis believes that homosexuals are born that way "because of their female hormones." Carlos believes it is something "genetic." Pedro feels that "chemical" changes are responsible. Others think "excessive petting and pampering" are the cause.

Inmates do associate *cacherismo* with environmental factors: masculine men who practice sodomy do so "for lack of women," according to José. "Because of a need to have sex," says Toro, or "just for the hell of it." Or because they have nothing better to do, as Carlos Alberto says. Because this behavior is the result of environment and extreme circumstances, the inmates do not regard it as an illness or as something out of the ordinary. "Men need to use their dick to feel like men, and if they don't have a woman, then they screw a guy," explains Enrique. "You become a *cachero* because of circumstances. But if I had women, I wouldn't look for gays," says Chino.

In view of the power that they wield, the sexual discourse of the *cacheros* predominates in prison. The homosexuals themselves accept that their lovers are not gay, and do not have much in common with them. For their part, the transvestites accept that they are, in practice, women. Part of this acceptance is an acknowledgement of the low value women have in a *machista* society. The transvestites must wash, cook, clean, and sweep the "house," the niche or den where they live with their "man."

The essentialist view of homosexuality and the perception that only passive individuals are homosexuals means that the *cacheros* are more tolerant of gays. Unlike the prison staff, inmates do not blame homosexuality on families, parents, or economic circumstances. They believe it is a disease people are born with and that it is unfair to blame them for it. "I think gays are born that way," says Chino, "and nothing can be done to change them. Why ask them to be different?" Daniel believes that homosexuality is "genetic" and that it is wrong "to make them feel bad for being that way." Toro shares the view that gays are really "women" who are "born" that way, and people should respect them.

Chapter 2

The *Cachero* and the Transvestite

Prison is an institution full of contradictions: on one hand, there is great tolerance of homosexuality, and on the other, there is a masculine culture that is aggressive and hostile toward anything that is weak or feminine. To survive, inmates must learn to defend themselves and protect their space. For this reason, physical strength and skill in the use of knives and other sharp weapons are indispensable.

It is possible to characterize various types of homosexual couples:

    a. The *cachero* and the transvestite.
    b. The older man and the *güila* or *kid*.
    c. Two in-the-closet homosexuals, known as "foxes."
    d. Combinations of all the above.

In this culture, which places greater value on masculinity, homosexual relations are tolerated provided certain basic rules concerning sexual roles are respected. An effeminate and weak individual may establish a relationship with a *cachero*—a man who is masculine and who does not "officially" define himself as a homosexual. The first presents himself socially as a woman and the second as a man. To keep the roles separate, the homosexual or transvestite always uses a woman's name, dresses as such, and performs "feminine" tasks for the *cachero*: ironing, washing, cleaning. The latter, when talking about his lover with other inmates, always refers to his partner as "she." The relationship also includes the protection that the *cachero* provides his lover. He protects the transvestite from the advances of other men.

In theory, the *cachero* is the one who penetrates, and the gay is the one who is penetrated. *Cacherismo* is defined by the relationship of a man who penetrates a homosexual. A *cachero* must not serve another man, as a woman does, according to Luis. "Serving" means allowing oneself to be penetrated. The male who possesses another male is considered a "man" or heterosexual, provided his active role is made obvious. However, in practice, this polarization is more complex, as we shall see later.

"Who are the *cacheros?*" we ask Toro. "To be a *cachero*, first of all you have to be very masculine, no feathers," he replies. "You also have to have money in jail. A poor *cachero* isn't a *cachero*," he adds. "And how do you make money in jail?" we ask. "Well, usually by dealing drugs, liquor, services, or food," he replies. *Cacheros* are generally *coles* (powerful inmates who control the money), gang leaders, guys who control others and who control the lives of everyone in jail." "So being a *cachero* and a *col* is almost the same thing?" we ask. "Well, almost the same. There's always a *col* who doesn't like sodomy and doesn't have a lover, and there are also *cacheros* who aren't *coles*, but in general they're almost the same thing," Toro tells us.

The *cachero* is attracted by the femininity of the transvestite. For him, the more mannered and the closer to being a woman a transvestite is, the more attractive she is. That is why many *cacheros* require transvestites to shave their legs, wear makeup, and let their hair grow long. Although they are forbidden to dress as women in jail, the transvestites do their best to look like women. For them, the attraction of the *cachero* lies in his masculinity and aggressiveness. Transvestites usually choose *cacheros* for their strength and good looks, as well as for the size of their sexual organs. The *cacheros* admit that the transvestites check them out in the shower to "evaluate the size." Other reasons for seeking out *cacheros* are the protection they offer, and sometimes money. However, more often than not, the transvestites end up subsidizing the vices of their lovers. "Toro," we ask, "why do transvestites go for a big penis?" He looks at us with a certain condescension and replies confidently: "The prostate is the answer." "The prostate?" we ask without understanding his meaning. "Well, men have it and women don't. It's one of the strongest sexual organs that exist. When it's stimulated, you feel pleasure on both sides. That's why the size of the penis is important for the transvestites and the queers, and not so much for women. The deeper it goes, the more pleasure and the more stimulus to the prostate. Women, on the other hand, get more pleasure in the clitoris than in the vagina."

Despite their obvious femininity, the transvestites, like the *cacheros*, are men with a great propensity for infidelity. Unlike the kids, the transvestites enjoy sexual relations, whether for love or for money. For this reason, they try to make the largest possible number of conquests and try not to miss out on the handsome and masculine prisoners. This goes against the type of relationship to which *cacheros* are accustomed. Because the *cacheros* had relationships only with women before entering prison, they are more accustomed to a double standard: their women must be faithful to them. But this fidelity is not easy to find in the transvestites, especially among those who normally prostitute themselves. "Transvestites are worse than whores. Whores have sex without feeling desire, but transvestites really enjoy every fuck. It's much harder to sexually satisfy a transvestite than a whore," says Toro.

INITIATION

How does a man who has been heterosexual all his life begin to feel an attraction to another man? In fact, there are as many paths as situations. In prison, inmates are removed from daily contact with women, except for a few female prison officials or conjugal visits. It is therefore practically impossible to establish an emotional relationship with a woman. At the same time, homosexual relations are more open. Little by little, the desire to have sex and the activity of fellow inmates begins to have an effect on many prisoners.

In one of the courses run by ILPES for volunteers who wish to work in prisons, the following exercise is used by instructors to make them understand how sexual attraction to other men can develop in a heterosexual man:

> Close your eyes slowly and focus on your breathing for a few minutes. Inhale and exhale. Don't think about anything other than the slow and relaxed rhythm of your own breathing. Inhale and exhale.

When you are totally relaxed, you're going to imagine that you've been in jail for three years. Using your imagination, visualize yourself sitting in a prison mess hall, like any of the ones we know. Think, you've been locked up for three years in this place, which is now familiar to you. Think for a few moments about this situation.

Now that you imagine yourself sitting alone in this big mess hall, you recall that you've been here for more than three years. Nobody has touched you or kissed you or made love to you in all this time. You feel kind of sad and despondent.

Suddenly, the room fills up with three or four hundred women [if the participants are women] or men [if the participants are men]. There are all types of men or women: tall, short, fat, thin, muscular, flaccid, attractive, ugly. You stop and look at the great variety of types that are there.

If you're a woman, you stop to look at a strange but very attractive girl who is sitting in front of you. She has no breasts, her body is well-built, almost muscular, and her face is beautiful but masculine. Her teeth are white, her lips are full, like those of an Italian actor. Suddenly she looks at you and smiles.

If you're a man, imagine that among the group of men in front of your table there is a very pretty, feminine-looking man. He has breasts, his lips are painted a light red color, his hair is blond and curly, he has a narrow waist and a woman's legs. Suddenly he looks at you and smiles.

Now think that you like this person. Forget, for a minute, about the person's sex. Your fellow inmates, noticing the flirtation, encourage you to get to know each other. "How lucky to get a response from that beautiful person," some friends tell you. People seem to celebrate the attraction.

Now, I want you ask yourself how you feel. What pulls you toward that person? Do you like him/her? Do you think it's possible to have something with him/her?

Once you've thought about this, you will begin to return to the place where we began the exercise. You will become aware of your body, move your hands and feet around, and when I count to three, you will open your eyes.

The volunteers accept that the exercise helps them to understand how a person can develop an attraction for someone of the same sex. Maria, a sociologist, tells us, "Yes, I was able to feel an attraction for one of the women in the prison. I imagined her to be well built, a little rough but beautiful, and I felt so alone that I needed to be with her and even needed to kiss her." Leonardo, a psychologist, says he imagined "a very beautiful transvestite, slim, tall, and sensual. I forgot he had a penis; I didn't care." Others were unable to do the exercise and some did not feel any attraction. However, the exercise serves to illustrate the possibilities in prison: some can substitute a person of the same sex for one of the opposite sex, if they are heterosexual, while others cannot do so at all, and those who are homosexual have a ball. "Being in jail is like being put in a disco all day, with free food and a bed, and men who are all turned on," a homosexual says. "Well, these are the same choices that are available in jail," the instructor tells us.

Toro and Angelita are a typical example of a *cachero*-transvestite relationship. The first is heterosexual and had his first sexual experience with an older female cousin. As is often the case, Toro's cousin, who was almost eleven years older than he was, sexually abused him when he was only ten years old. Toro had sexual relations with this cousin for several months and she taught him about oral and vaginal sex. Then he began to seduce other women. Toro is an extremely attractive man and admits he has "great power over women." However, his addiction to drugs led him to begin dealing and eventually he landed in jail. Until then, Toro had never had homosexual relations. He does not like men and likes even less to be "used like a woman," he tells us. "If anyone ever dares to touch me behind, I'll kill him," he says firmly.

However, Toro met Angelita, a transvestite who injects herself with hormones, has breasts, and is extremely feminine. When Toro looks at her he experiences something very strange. He knows Angelita is a man, but he embarked upon a new relationship:

Interviewer: Could you tell me a little about Angelita and how you met?

Toro: Well, when I was in here—one of the many times I've been inside—in a wing where most of the homosexuals are admitted. They were shouting "bu-bu" because a new prisoner was arriving. From the moment I saw him come in, I was attracted to him; I liked him a whole lot, and so from then on we began a friendship and talked about everything. And I knew right away that this homosexual found me attractive and that he liked me, because I liked him and when he visited he would come over and say, "Here, you want to get stoned?" and so forth. Then one day he was released, and he called me every day. That time nothing happened but he was jailed a second time and the flirtation continued.

Interviewer: Was he dressed like a woman?

Toro: No, he came dressed in men's clothes, because they don't allow them to come in here in women's clothes. They arrive like that, but outside they change their clothes. But he had long hair, completely smooth legs, a round, shapely backside, narrow waist, and a totally sensual mouth. Any man would be attracted by so much femininity. There was a third time when he was in jail and I remember it very well. I was handing out refreshments when I saw him come in, but he didn't see me. So when I was handing out the refreshments I saw that when he passed through the gates he asked some inmates, "Where does Toro sleep?" and they told him where my bed was, and I continued giving out the refreshments and all the guys began to tease me, "Hey, Toro, look what's arrived for you" and other stupid remarks. I went to my bed and he said, "Can I stay here?" and I said, "Sure, you're welcome! It's my bed and yours too." Angelita told me that he'd seen me bathing and that I had a very big, thick penis. Half an hour later, we'd already had our first sexual encounter and the relationship continued for three months and she would tell me that she loved me—I call him "her" because it's the way I like it, I don't like to treat her as the man she is—she told me that she loved me, etc., that she had found the man of her dreams, of her life. But I didn't believe her, because I said that as soon as she left, I wouldn't exist and that maybe it was something fleeting and she told me no, never, and that she wouldn't leave me for anything in the world, that she would always stand by me, and she swore this to me and said that only death would separate us. I said to myself, "That's fine." She was released, went to trial, and kept calling me and would come to all the visiting days, and every day she would send me something and would often call me on the phone and ask me what I needed and this and that and so on.

Martínez had a different kind of initiation. He is thirty-three years old and all his previous relationships were heterosexual:

Interviewer: Tell me a little about your sexual relationships prior to going to jail, about your childhood, your adolescence. What kind of sexual relationships did you have? What were they like? How did you begin?

Martínez: Sexually, I began at fourteen. No, thirteen. I was a ticket collector on the San Juan de Dios bus, and I met my first woman and she was about thirty-three or thirty-four and I had sex with her. I learned from her during the seven or eight years we lived together. That's where my sexual relationships began and to this day, I've always had great lays, as they say , and it's been like that continuously and now I've been alone for two years, but I lived with around fifteen or sixteen women.

Martínez has been in prison for seventeen years and had never had previous homosexual relations. When he entered prison, he had no idea that "two men could have sex" and he was "repelled" by the idea of homosexual sex. However, the passing of the years had their effect. He admits that "life in prison had gotten me used to this world and I've hung out with young kids who are real gays." When asked how he defines "gays," he answers that they are males who do not like having sex with women because they have "female hormones." A month and a half ago, he had a transvestite for a cellmate. The homosexual was assigned the bunk bed just under Martínez. One night he heard strange sounds coming from the bed underneath: "I was sleeping when I heard the queer moaning. When I woke up, I realized that the black guy, Tulipan, was making love to him. I'd seen similar things in jail, so it was nothing new. But the conversation I heard this time really turned me on." When we asked him what was so unusual about this conversation, he said, "It was a very affectionate relationship between the two. Tulipan is famous for his size and he's cut up more than one person. But this time, he was calming the guy down, and persuading him to let himself be loved." Martínez was so impressed by this dialogue that two nights later he himself climbed into his companion's bed and said, "I know what you like. I'm going to love you like Tulipan." However, Martínez found it difficult to accept the idea that he was having a homosexual relationship:

>**Interviewer:** What you're saying now is that you have a lover here in jail?
>
>**Martínez:** Yes, that's right.
>
>**Interviewer:** Talk to me a little about what makes you feel guilty.
>
>**Martínez:** Guilty in the sense that I have intercourse with a person of the same sex.
>
>**Interviewer:** Do you think that's bad?
>
>**Martínez:** Well, as far as the Bible and God are concerned, it's bad.
>
>**Interviewer:** Tell me a bit about your partner. Is he a transvestite, a fox, or a kid?
>
>**Martínez:** No, he's gay, a transvestite, like a woman. He has . . . how should I say?
>
>**Interviewer:** Breasts?
>
>**Martínez:** Yes, breasts; he's gay.
>
>**Interviewer:** How long have you been together?
>
>**Martínez:** About a month and a half, more or less.

Interviewer: And you feel good about this relationship?

Martínez: Well, yes and no. I'm intimate with him; I like to talk, you know, maybe because he's the person next to me, who's joined to me in many ways in prison, who respects my opinion, respects what I am, without saying a word.

Interviewer: Tell me a little about what your relationship is like with this person, with your partner. When you have sexual relations with her are you aware that she's a man? Can you talk to me a little, if it doesn't bother you, about what you do, without getting into a pornographic description? How do you feel knowing that she has a penis?

Martínez: Well, I feel bad, obviously, because like I said, my sexual initiation was with women. I've known him for a month and a half—well, five months—and he has a very special way of being, so I don't feel bad. But I feel bad because he's a man just like me.

Chino, a muscular man of forty-two, has been in prison twice. He has four children and lives with a woman. Like many other men, he was sexually initiated by an older woman:

Interviewer: How were you initiated into sex?

Chino: When I had school vacations, I would go to my family's house. An aunt was the one who initiated me into sexual activities.

Interviewer: How old were you?

Chino: Seven or eight.

Interviewer: And your aunt?

Chino: She might have been fifteen or sixteen. She was already a grown woman. She had pubic hair, enormous breasts, and she would masturbate against my leg and I'd get an erection.

Interviewer: What happened with her?

Chino: I began to touch her. I liked to touch her breasts, always afraid of her "thing," because I was still a kid. I was still wet behind the ears, as people say, I was scared. She would grab me and masturbate . . .

Chino went to prison for the first time at the age of nineteen, to the old Central Penitentiary. Here he met many homosexuals and began having sex with men. However, his sexual encounters, as he himself says, are "for the hell of it," in other words, just to satisfy himself sexually. Unlike Toro or Martínez, Chino does not complicate his life with love. His main reason for mixing with homosexuals is simply satisfaction. When asked about his first experience, he says, "It was three in the morning. I'd been in jail for three months. It was a very hot night and there was a queer with a nice ass who liked me. I imagined that I was with a girlfriend I knew, I closed my eyes and I began to fly."

Interviewer: Have you had a man in jail when you've been imprisoned?

Chino: Well, to tell the truth, yes of course I've had a partner, who has been like a woman to me.

Interviewer: Tell me as much as you can about this person.

Chino: Well, he's a submissive person, always willing to serve me whenever I need it, obeys me in everything, doesn't look at other men who want to fuck him, isn't unfaithful, is quite jealous. He's a complete lady, not a bitch or a whore like you could call other types of homosexuals who sleep with you, and even though you might be their husband, they go with other people behind your back.

Interviewer: This person is with you now, or was that some time ago?

Chino: No, that was a long time ago, when I was in jail, because I don't go in for those practices when I'm outside.

Interviewer: Did you gradually become a *cachero* in the Peni [Penitentiary]? What was the process of becoming a *cachero* like and how did you begin to practice *cacherismo*?

Chino: I began to practice *cacherismo* with a friend who was a homosexual.

Interviewer: A transvestite?

Chino: Yes, a transvestite. But we didn't do penetration, just masturbation. He would masturbate me and, you know, do certain sexual caresses.

Interviewer: How many sexual relationships have you had during your time in jail?

Chino: I couldn't say exactly, but many.

Juan Alberto is one of the few inmates who had experienced sexual relations with transvestites before going to prison. His first sexual relationship was accidental. Juan Alberto was tricked:

Interviewer: Tell me something, have you had relations with transvestites, with men who dress as women?

Juan Alberto: Sure I have, here in Alajuela, with Aurora, a gay from the north. I saw him one day when I went to a certain bar and saw him dressed like a woman with a friend that I later found out was the president of an organization of queens in Alajuela. I decided to have a few drinks, and then we went downtown in a taxi and he took me to a room somewhere. And, well, I had thought she was a woman but when I saw her without clothes, I said to myself, "Wow, this is a man!" It was Aurora and I had a little affair with him. It was a nice experience, because even when you've been around, it's nice to have different affairs and experiences, both with women and with men. For me that's something very normal.

Interviewer: I imagine that when you arrived in prison, a whole new world opened up in terms of sexuality. Maybe you were familiar with it, maybe not. Can you tell me a little about this sexual world?

Juan Alberto: Yeah, well, when I came into the prison system for the first time, to the admission unit, it was a different world than what I was used to. The first time I was in prison, in "A" block, I was kind of doubtful because people said there were a lot of diseases, AIDS and all that, but when I came here I saw a world which is what we're living in now, where there are so many homosexuals, all kinds of people. Later, I was in "H" block, where I had a relationship with a gay called Laura, and, well, for me, it was a normal affair. Of course, I took care of myself, because people said this gay was infected with AIDS, but what I did then was to use a condom. . . .

There are many other forms of initiation. Pedro's attraction to transvestites began when he participated in a gang rape. According to him, "It never occurred to me to have sex with a gay. But my gang had to punish one of them. We lined up to fuck him, and when it was my turn, it felt fantastic. The next time I did it with that gay, I did it for pleasure." Others, like Carlos, were seduced by the transvestites themselves. Once, while he was bathing, he was approached by one of them:

> I was bathing and this queen, Carrasqueri, came up. I didn't suspect what he was coming for. He began to writhe like a female. He was a kind of half-caste guy and looked like Michael Jackson. He would put the soap between his breasts and glance at me out of the corner of his eye. Then he would turn around and soap himself like a real hot chick. I noticed that he had put on black leather underpants and a ring through his tongue. When I saw all that camp stuff I got a hard-on. The queen saw that I was excited and said, "You're a real hunk." The guy knelt down and I let him suck me. Then he took off his pants and, with a lot of moaning, he guided my dick into him.

The initiations described by the *cacheros* prove that human sexuality is more flexible than we might imagine. The inmates are subjected to a truly extreme situation because of the absence of women.

However, *cacheros* are not forced into sexual relations with other men. Attraction develops to varying degrees and at different times. In some cases, it does not develop at all. There are some inmates who never have any sexual involvement with other men. Despite living in the same conditions as the rest, they never develop a taste for homosexuality. This is the case with Mario:

> I have nothing against gays. In fact, I can tell you that one of the ones who defended me was, as they say, gay. As a professional he was pretty bad, because he graduated when he was already quite old and I think I got more time in jail because of his lack of experience. They called him the "white granny" because he was gray-haired and had kids. But as a person he was a very cool guy. Instead of charging me, he said I should pay him "in kind," as he himself referred to sex. But I told him that though I have nothing against gays, I don't like sodomy. I never let him touch me. Since I came here, many "boyfriends" have come on to me, but I tell them I'm not interested. However turned on I am, I can't find anything that I like in a man. Even less among the transvestites who are horrible by day and really ugly at night. One of those queens came up to me one day and asked if I liked her. I said, "Look, honey, you're so feminine that you look more like a feminine lesbian." From that moment, the queen doesn't even come near me.

SEXUAL PRACTICES

In theory, *cacheros* are the "machos," the penetrators in the sexual relationship. A series of rules determines what can and cannot be done. One of these rules is that the macho should not allow himself to be penetrated and should not play with the transvestite's penis. Another rule is that he should not perform passive oral sex or kiss the transvestite on the mouth. Toro is an example of the traditional *cachero.*

Interviewer: Could you tell me a little about the type of sexual relationship you had with Angelita?

Toro: Well, at first I myself couldn't believe what I was doing. She's the only homosexual person I've been with. At first, I didn't know how to do it, because before I had the idea that the creature who was in bed with me had the same thing that I had.

Interviewer: What was that?

Toro: A pair of testicles and a penis. And I couldn't get used to that, because from the waist up, it was a woman's body, with breasts, long hair, fine features, but from the waist down I still couldn't understand it, and with all the caresses and the groping, I always avoided that area. Every time I thought about it, it bothered me, but in time I got used to it.

Interviewer: When did you confront the fact that Angelita is a man?

Toro: Well, I knew she was a man from the beginning, but my body felt some vibrations, like what a man feels when he falls in love with a woman. And the third time she came in here, she came into my den, to live with me, and the relationship began and it continued, and I still had that fear of being with another man. "He's got the same thing I have," I'd say to myself, and then, during masturbation, during sodomy, and during foreplay I always avoided the testicles and the penis.

Interviewer: You didn't touch them?

Toro: No, and the relationship grew stronger every day, for three months, and then she left and she's always kept on supporting me to this day.

Interviewer: What did you feel when you had a woman from the waist up and a man from the waist down? How did your life change?

Toro: I learned something I didn't know. When we made love, I didn't see the person masturbate or anything. I simply remember that in the moment that I was coming, the guy, without being excited or anything, at the moment he noticed that I was coming, he was doing the same, and I couldn't understand why. And later I asked him, and he said that was his satisfaction, because with other men he'd needed to masturbate, but not with me. That made me feel very manly, because I learned that only big penises can massage the prostate so deeply that the person doesn't even need to touch himself to have an orgasm. It was very beautiful to learn that and it makes me very proud.

However, Toro himself admits that familiarity has led him to make changes.

Interviewer: Do you caress Angelita's penis now?

Toro: Yes, over time I began to do that.

Interviewer: So you've changed?

Toro: Yes, one changes completely. I realized that she loved me and I loved her and I went for a year without doing anything different, until later I became used to it. But only up to a certain point, because I'll never let her penetrate me, and I won't perform oral sex on her.

Interviewer: You won't do that?

Toro: No, I suck her breasts and her backside, her buttocks, anything except the penis.

Interviewer: Do you think you'll ever get to do that?

Toro: I don't know.

Many *cacheros* make more changes than Toro. In prison there is a saying that "an old rooster ends up getting fucked," which means that after constantly penetrating transvestites, the *cachero* is curious to find out what it feels like, and so he "gives his ass," as Daniel says. In other words, the macho man decides to let himself be penetrated out of curiosity. However, very few of the interviewees admit to having done this, though they are willing to recognize it in others. Daniel tells us that *cacheros* become bored with penetrating homosexuals: "I know a couple and at night the moans of pain alternate. First it's the gay that gets laid. But then you hear the other one saying, "Not so hard." Joaquín says the same about several of his friends. "The *cacheros*, who are so macho, eat it, as we say around here. In other words, they kill the ox [sit on the other person's penis]. There are loads of them." This has become so common that it is often seen. According to Luis, he himself found two masculine men penetrating each other. "When I went to the bathroom, I saw them and I couldn't believe it. I said, 'Go ahead, I didn't see a thing.'"

Proof of this sexual flexibility may be seen in the answers to the questions on sexual practices given by the twenty-two transvestites we interviewed in 1989. Despite the polarization of gender roles, in sexual practice there is a greater symmetry, since the *cacheros*, or supposed heterosexuals, practice active or passive anal sex with their transvestite lovers. On average, the transvestites have a greater possibility of active anal penetration when they are in a closed relationship with a *cachero*.

The transvestites themselves admit, in the workshops, that the *cacheros* sometimes change roles; in other words, they allow themselves to be penetrated, and also perform active and passive oral sex. Felicia explains, "After so many times of seeing the pleasure felt by the queens, the man is curious to know what it's like and how it feels. Little by little, they dare to allow someone to penetrate them." Laura says she is popular among the *cacheros* because "I have a big dick. If they were only active," she continues, "do you think they would care?" Others learn to perform oral sex. Carmen has been in a relationship with her *cachero* for two years and he has changed his way of making love. "Before, he was so macho that he wouldn't even touch my penis. Now he's like a lamb."

The passive sexual act of a *cachero* could be interpreted as a more liberal attitude and a greater respect for his sexual partner. However, it is not. Unlike the symmetry found in relationships between "foxes," which we shall examine later, the *cacheros* are doing nothing revolutionary by their passivity. On the contrary, the fact that a *cachero* allows himself to be penetrated rather demonstrates how much of a *cachero* he is: he can give himself the luxury of allowing himself to be penetrated by slaves, soldiers, and subalterns. We ask Daniel if a *cachero* loses power by giving his ass. "Never! A *cachero* has power because he controls the gangs or the money. If he gives his ass, it's a personal matter. Nobody makes a move to knock him off his perch. Who will dare to challenge Pico Malo, who has killed four people, because once in a while he gives his ass?"

CACHERO *LOVE*

Once a *cachero* and a transvestite have begun a liaison, the relationship may develop along very different paths. In some cases, they become a couple, in theory no different from a heterosexual couple. A de facto marriage takes place, with all the rules of the game in terms of fidelity, companionship, and the division of labor. This is the case with Toro and Angelita:

Interviewer: To summarize, you'd never had sexual relations with a man before?

Toro: Never.

Interviewer: Until you met Angelita.

Toro: Until I met her.

Interviewer: And knowing Angelita has made you change your life?

Toro: Totally, maybe because of the way she is. I was baptized by the Church, I have two daughters from one marriage. I was divorced and then married in a civil wedding and have another son and others along the way. But after I met Angelita everything changed. The rest was another phase of my life, I was beginning something new, totally separate.

Interviewer: Have you been faithful to Angelita?

Toro: A hundred percent.

Interviewer: What have you learned about homosexuality here in jail?

Toro: I don't know, I met the person who lives with me here and from the first moment I saw her, I loved her. I was one of the ones who used to say: "Me gay? Me a queer? Never!" However, someone came along and I've been with her for nearly six years. And we keep struggling along together, visit after visit. She comes to see me and then there's all the telephone calls, which is what encourages me to keep going. Because really, I've learned more about the reality of love with this transvestite than when I was with women, more than with the woman who is the mother of my two daughters. My other ex-wife, the one who's the mother of my son, I see as garbage, but with this transvestite I've found many things that I never found in a great number of women who've been to bed with me.

In some cases, the relationship remains distant. The *cachero* uses his companion but does not love him or live with him as a couple. This is precisely Chino's situation:

Interviewer: How did you express your feelings toward him? Did you love him? Were you affectionate? Explain your feelings toward him.

Chino: Well, a humanitarian feeling, always treating him well, but not loving him or desiring him, or falling madly in love, but more than anything it's a way of getting rid of the tensions that you need to release. Over time, I came to the conclusion that it's not just for the hell of it, but because you really need it, you want it because it's a physical need, because you get that urge to have an orgasm.

Chapter 3

The *Cachero* and the Kid

Another type of relationship that is tolerated in the culture of prison inmates is that between an older man and a younger man, known as a *güila* or a *cabrito* (a kid). Young prisoners are sought after by those who have been in prison for a long time, and who seek a relationship of control and "female" services, in exchange for protection inside the jail. Although the gender difference is not so marked in this type of relationship, the seniority of age allows the older man to consider himself the macho and the protector of the younger, weaker man, replicating a heterosexual relationship.

Cachero-güila relationships differ from those involving transvestites. In the first place, the *cachero* who seeks out young men is attracted by the age, not the affectation or mannerisms of his partner. In general, the *güilas* are masculine-looking young men. Moreover, they are not homosexuals and are not attracted to men. The "homosexualization" of the *güilas* is a process that may take days, weeks, or years.

One of the advantages that *cacheros* see in *güilas* is that they are more faithful, since they are not attracted to other men. According to Daniel, *cacheros* believe that *güilas* are less promiscuous than transvestites. Luis tells us that "you won't find a *güila* ogling a *cachero* in the shower to see what his penis is like, like the transvestites do." Ernesto believes that *güilas* remain content with their man." *Cacheros* who look for *güilas* are generally pedophiles. Daniel and his son, who is in prison with him, are an example.

Interviewer: Do you like young boys?

Daniel: Yes.

Interviewer: What about those older than you?

Daniel: Yes, I've had older ones, but I like young ones.

Interviewer: And young girls of that age?

Daniel: Young girls also.

Interviewer: You like them too?

Daniel: Yes.

Interviewer: You like both?

Daniel: Yes, I've had young girls of fifteen or sixteen.

Interviewer: But you have a preference for young boys?

Daniel: Yes, male love is better.

Interviewer: Male love is better?

Daniel: Yes, it's better.

Interviewer: Do you always pay them?

Daniel: Yes, of course, I always give them money.

Interviewer: How does that work here in jail?

Daniel: You pay here too, always, of course. But here it's cheaper than on the street, around 300 or 500 colones.

Interviewer: Have you had lasting relationships with women? Marriage or girlfriends?

Daniel: No, only girlfriends.

Interviewer: Have you lived with a woman?

Daniel: No, but I went out with a girl and I fucked her.

Interviewer: In other words, you like both things.

Daniel: Yes, but now I'm into *cacherismo* more than anything. It works better, because it's very tough in jail.

Interviewer: Do you have children?

Daniel: Yes, I have five children.

Interviewer: How old are they?

Daniel: The eldest is twenty-four, another is eighteen, and another seventeen. The youngest are fifteen and sixteen.

Interviewer: You never had sexual relations with your children?

Daniel: Oh no! I respect them a lot.

Interviewer: Are any of them homosexual?

Daniel: Yes, one of them turned out the same as me.

Interviewer: Son or daughter?

Daniel: Son.

Interviewer: Is he a *cachero*?

Daniel: Yes.

Interviewer: How old is he?

Daniel: Twenty-four, and he's one hell of a *cachero*!

Interviewer: How do you know?

Daniel: I know because I've seen him.

Interviewer: Tell me about that.

Daniel: He's an inmate in the jail where I was.

Interviewer: You're sure he's a *cachero*?

Daniel: Yes.

Interviewer: You saw him do it?

Daniel: Yes, he was with me there, and when he was by my side I saw him in action.

Interviewer: Did the two of you talk about these things?

Daniel: Yes.

Interviewer: Did you compare men?

Daniel: Yes.

Interviewer: Have you shared *güilas*?

Daniel: Yes, of course.

Interviewer: When you were in jail?

Daniel: Yes.

Interviewer: That's very interesting, and I'd like us to talk some more about that. You say that you've shared sexual partners with your son in jail?

Daniel: Yes, of course.

Interviewer: Tell me about that.

Daniel: After I was done with him [the *güila*], I passed him on to my son, and well, he would carry on doing great. And he'd say "Dad, I turned out just like you."

Interviewer: Do you feel guilty about that?

Daniel: No, but I'm to blame: he's the same as me because one day he saw me.

Interviewer: He saw you in the jail?

Daniel: Yes, and he said he wanted to know about those things. I said if he wanted to learn I'd pass the *güilas* on to him, after I'd used them, and so we shared them. After one of us finishes having sex with a *güila*, the other takes him and fucks him. My son told me that he's proud to have learned with me.

Interviewer: Have you sat down to compare notes—in other words, do you tell each other about how you felt and what you did?

Daniel: Yes, he's told me things. He says how great it is, that it's better than with a woman, it's tighter because women are more loose and men are tighter, and that sex with men feels better, and well, we both like it.

Interviewer: And do you feel good about your relationship with your son, do you get along?

Daniel: Yes, we get along well.

Interviewer: Do you like your partners to be transvestites, to be dressed like women, or not?

Daniel: Oh no! I like them to be serious.

Interviewer: What do you mean by "serious"?

Daniel: Manly.

Interviewer: You don't like having sex with *güilas* who are queens or effeminate?

Daniel: Oh no, not the effeminate ones, because they go around with everyone. But the straight ones are different, they don't make love with everybody, mainly because of the diseases, because some go around with this one and that one. That's why, if you have a *güila*, he'd better be faithful.

Interviewer: Are you faithful to him?

Daniel: Yes.

Interviewer: You only go with him?

Daniel: Just with him.

Interviewer: You don't think that a faithful *güila* can also pass on a disease?

Daniel: Yes, of course. That's why when I'm going to make love, I check him out first.

Interviewer: How do you check him out?

Daniel: Well, to see how much he's screwed, because I've been doing this for eighteen years, and I grab him, open him up and put my finger up him to see how he is. The ones who are infected have a kind of strange smell and you know they're infected.

Other *cacheros* have developed a taste for young men while in prison. Carlos, for example, used to like girls under fifteen. His passion was to go off with the girls and "play house" with them. When we asked him to describe the game, he said he would ask the girls to "play the role of mother" and he would "play father." The girls, without suspecting his intentions, would gradually become more trusting and little by little would yield to his demands. "One day, I ask them to pretend that we go to sleep together. Another time, we pretend to examine each other's bodies. Before they know it, I've possessed them." While in jail, Carlos looks for whoever most closely resembles a young girl. "Well, here you don't have any chance of finding little girls. The only thing you see here are the female prison officers who are more wide open than the Zurqui tunnel [a large tunnel on one of Costa Rica's main highways]. I enjoy getting acquainted with the *güilas* who come here and playing around with them." This is a complicated game that goes on for months:

> Many of these kids are criminals but they're innocent about sodomy. When a little blond, white-skinned kid arrives, all beardless and hairless, I gradually befriend him. I offer him food and cigarettes. I invite him to stay with me in my den. At night, I touch him on the sly, like I didn't really mean to do it. If I see that he doesn't say anything, the next time I grab him deliberately. Little by little I begin to masturbate him. In one or two months, I begin playing around behind. I do this very carefully, because the kid doesn't know how to do this. First I insert a finger, that's all. . . . In a few more weeks he's mine.

Others, such as Teja, began as *cacheros* with transvestites and gradually developed a taste for young men. He says that before he met Ana, he had never seen a transvestite. However, a "kid with a big ass" was assigned the bunk below his. The young man was not a homosexual but a *güila* who was visited by another *cachero*. Teja could not help but be impressed by what he saw:

> I have a lot of respect for Calderón, because he's a very manly, butch type, a real thug, but one night I heard him begging the *güila* below me. First he gave him a crack joint so he'd get a good blast [get high]. Then I saw him get into the den and begin taking the kid's pants down. Looking down from above, I saw what pink, rounded buttocks that kid has. Wow! I like Ana's butt, but his was phenomenal. I heard when Calderón took the *güila*. The kid told him that he'd never had a banging [passive anal sex] of that quality. He said, "You squeezed all the juice out from inside, you motherfucker. Get out, I can't stand the pain." I was all turned on by this, and ever since that night I often thought about getting into his bed. Well, last week, the kid began to make eyes at me, because Calderón was moved to another block. I didn't waste any time and went down to him

and told him, "Look, if you go with me, you close down that little backside of yours. I don't want any more playing around." He said, "Well, I don't want to see you with Ana either. You either stay with that queen or come with me. . . ." So, I left Ana for this guy . . .

Luis is a very different case. He was raped by another man when he was just seven years old and decided to take his revenge by doing the same to boys that age:

Interviewer: Let's take it step by step. How did you come to be raped? What happened? Describe it in plenty of detail.

Luis: Well, that day I was home and I went for a walk in the village. I went into a cantina [a bar].

Interviewer: How old were you?

Luis: Seven.

Interviewer: You drank liquor at that age?

Luis: No, no, no. It wasn't that I drank liquor, but back then I liked to play with bottle caps, so I went in there. When I went into the bar, there was an older man, who was around thirty-five at the time. He was tall, thin, and bald and he asked me where San Vito was. I told him I knew and he said, "Can you take me there?" and I said, "Sure I can," and when we were walking along the railroad line, he grabbed me by the neck and covered my mouth and dragged me into an abandoned house. Once inside, he began taking my clothes off, he pulled my pants down and, well . . . there was penetration, in other words, he traumatized me.

Interviewer: When he'd finished with you, what happened? What did you do?

Luis: When he'd finished with me, he said we should go to San Vito and I said I didn't want to go. But he took me anyway, and kept kicking me behind, where it hurt. I walked along like I was all opened up and we arrived in San Vito where the fiestas were going on. He asked me if I wanted to eat something and I said no, nothing, that I wanted to go home. He told me I wasn't going home, that I was going to stay with him all day and who knows how many more days. And I said, "No, I want to go home." I was even crying by then, with tears in my eyes and with all that pain I felt. So I got into a car and got home, where my mother was, and she asked me where I'd been, and I said "around." I didn't have the courage to tell her, and as we've never been close enough to talk like mother to son, I didn't tell her what had happened that time.

This trauma led Luis to do the same to other children.

Interviewer: At that time you were seven—now we're going to move on a little. When was your first sexual experience with another man or young boy?

Luis: Well, around nine or ten, something like that.

Interviewer: Tell me what happened.

Luis: Well, with the resentment I felt because of what happened to me, I began to hate myself and I began to hate my classmates and friends. And as time went on, I grew up physically but emotionally I stayed the same.

Interviewer: When you say you hated yourself, what does that mean? That Luis hated Luis?

Luis: Exactly.

Interviewer: And you hated your friends?

Luis: Exactly.

Interviewer: Because of the memory of sexual abuse?

Luis: That's right, so the point came when I unloaded that hate on other smaller kids, who were six or seven years old. I'd go up to them to take them someplace, and I'd say, "Let's go for a walk," but I had all that filth in my mind.

Interviewer: How old were you?

Luis: I was about ten.

Interviewer: Did you penetrate them?

Luis: Yes.

Interviewer: Tell me about it.

Luis: Well, I would take them someplace. I would talk nicely to them and they would say no at first, but they would always come with me. When they took their clothes off, I would grab their anuses and begin to caress them, and then put a little saliva on it and penetrate them. Then they would yell and, to stop them from yelling too much, I would grab them by the neck with one hand and cover their mouth with the other so they wouldn't yell, so they wouldn't make a noise.

In jail, Luis continued this behavior against the *güilas*.

Interviewer: Do you think of yourself—if you wish to answer this—as a *güila*, a *cachero*, a fox, a transvestite, or none of these?

Luis: Well, I like to penetrate.

Interviewer: So, you're a *cachero* then?

Luis: Yes.

Interviewer: Tell me a little about yourself.

Luis: Well, I like penetration, because, I don't know, it's the sensation of penetrating the anus, not the vagina. Well, I like that too. But from behind, through the anus, it feels different. It reminds me of the old days, of past times, and that's why I began as a *cachero*, because as they did it to me, I learned how to do the same.

Interviewer: Do you have a *güila* here?

Luis: No, I don't.

Interviewer: Do you have sexual relations with some of the *güilas* here?

Luis: I've had sexual relations with some *güilas*.

Interviewer: Tell me about that.

Luis: Well, a lot of kids have asked me to please give them 300, 200, or 100 colones and I tell them I don't have any [money] and that what I have, I need. "What do you need it for?" they ask, and I tell them that it's to buy something. And then they end up saying that we should go to the bathroom so that I can give them a "drink" [semen] or penetrate them.

INITIATION

There are many ways of persuading a *güila* to agree to sexual relations. Some older *cacheros* who were imprisoned in San José's Central Penitentiary during the 1970s say that different tactics were used to subjugate inmates. Since prevention and education programs were nonexistent in the old penitentiary, prisoners were simply abandoned in their cells. Some of them would spend weeks or months without receiving visits, a situation *cacheros* would take advantage of to force some of the younger prisoners to have sex with them. Polo describes this as follows:

Things were very different before. In the Peni [San José's former prison], when a nice-looking *güila* arrived, they'd say a boat had come in, and he would be forced into a cell with several *cacheros*. He might be a tough small-time criminal; it didn't make any difference. They'd strip the guy, shave all of his body, powder him, and put him in a cell for three or four months without ever letting him out. Can you imagine what it's like to be used like a woman, day and night, by two or three guys for three months? Many of them ended up completely schizoid [schizophrenic]. You'd hear screams of pain during the day and at night from the penetrations they did to him. The *cacheros* would bring out the guy's underpants, which were red with blood, so everyone would laugh. It was a real joke! These kids would either go crazy or turn gay. Some of them would stay with just one guy to avoid being grabbed by the rest. I'll never forget Juancito, who was put in with a black guy who was famous in the Peni. I saw him in the shower and I saw the size of his dick. It was enormous! Well, the guy would screw Juancito, who ended up in the infirmary more than once. He asked me to protect him from the *cachero*, but I didn't want to have any problems. . . .

There is evidence that forced initiation continues. In the section on rape in Chapter 5, we shall see how many *güilas* are obliged to find themselves a *cachero* after being forced by several inmates. The young man learns to choose the lesser evil, which is to become the lover of a single "godfather." However, the appearance of crack in the country's jails, from the mid-1980s onward, has made things easier for the *cacheros*. Juan tells us that "it's not worth forcing" a young inmate if they're "willing to do anything for a hit of crack." This view is shared by Daniel, who says that "with money you can even buy a mother in jail." The need for money to buy highly addictive drugs means that "anyone will give his ass," says Teja. *Cacheros* simply need to introduce *güilas* to drugs and soon "they will do anything," says Tucan. "You don't need to complicate your life. I give them a few joints and I gradually tame them with drugs. They soon beg me to lend them money to buy more. Then I tell them that I want to see them naked to give them money. Finally, I've got them nailed and without saying a single word. Why should I complicate things with rape?"

Unlike the relationship between *cacheros* and transvestites, the *cachero-güila* relationship is characterized by its exclusivity. The *güilas* are generally under threat of death if they go with another *cachero*. Daniel makes it clear to his partners that the relationship is "'till death do us part." It is unusual to find a *güila* prostituting himself as openly as the transvestites do. In general, *cacheros* who go with *güilas* are the ones who provide the money, and not the other way round, as in the case of the transvestites. The fact that *güilas* are not homosexuals means that it is easier for them to be faithful to their partners. *Güilas* may end up enjoying sexual relations and even turn them around, and possess the *cacheros* themselves. However, they do not seek out men for their physical appearance, or for their virility, as the transvestites do, but rather for their money and their power.

THE GÜILA'S *STORY*

Juan Carlos is a *güila* who agreed to talk frankly to us. He describes the type of man he lives with, their relationship, their sexual practices, and their commitment to each other:

> **Interviewer:** You prefer to team up with an older person who can take care of you?
>
> **Juan Carlos:** Of course, because there are many older people here who are very respected. A young kid who's in here for swindling, say, isn't going to stand up for you if they try to knife you. On the other hand, an older person would, because most of the ones who are here are respected.
>
> **Interviewer:** Are they *coles*?
>
> **Juan Carlos:** Of course they are. I had an affair here with a guy like that. They called him José el Mago [the Magician]. He's been a *col* for a long time, of course. He's been in the Peni [the former prison of San José], doing time, and in San Lucas [a penitentiary located on an island in the Pacific Ocean]. And he's respected here in all the different sections, in medium security, and when I was having an affair and living with him, he told me not to worry, that if anything would

happen to me, first they would have to kill him and then me. He took care of me and defended me. I had an affair with that guy who was a *col*.

Interviewer: And did you enjoy it?

Juan Carlos: Yes, of course.

Interviewer: How old was he?

Juan Carlos: He was thirty.

Interviewer: Thirty is young, isn't it?

Juan Carlos: Yes, he was young, but he was very respected, because he was doing time for six homicides, with a thirty-two-year sentence. I was with him for a long while and he would take care of me and help me and give me advice all about the prison system here, how you have to coexist with the other inmates, and how to relate to different people, so that you don't have friction, or problems with them, you know, how to avoid those things, to keep away from certain people. Because here most people, if they see you with money, or they see you with drugs or something, they pretend to be friends at that moment but later, if you have any kind of problem, they turn their backs on you. They're not going to defend you.

Interviewer: I've noticed, and it occurs to me, that here there's a strong relationship between sex and death. In other words, the great *cacheros* have been killers. What can you tell me about that?

Juan Carlos: Well, the majority of those *cacheros* have turned into killers because they've had someone living with them, they've lent them money and had sex with them believing that they would have them always. But there comes a time when the *güila* leaves him and then he hears rumors that he's with someone else, making love and all that, and so the *cachero* gets jealous and immediately kills him. That's happened down here. They killed that queer, Corina, and La Tapa was killed for that, because of the jealousy of the *cachero,* who killed him over there in B1.

Interviewer: Continuing with the subject of jealousy and *cacherismo*, tell me a little about the people who slash themselves. Do you think there's any connection between people who slash their wrists, sex, and jealousy?

Juan Carlos: Of the people here, most of the ones who get into slashing themselves, nearly 20 percent do it because of drugs, because they don't have the money to buy dope, so they find a way to cut themselves. Another does it out of jealousy, because he wants a kid and, who knows, maybe the kid doesn't play ball, the kid's already splitting from him and others are courting him, so that person inflicts wounds on himself, that's what happens.

Interviewer: Recently you yourself were cut up, you cut your arm and I saw you about a week ago with several wounds. Did you do that because you felt hurt by someone, or some *cachero* hurt you, or a *güila* hurt you?

Juan Carlos: It was because the *cachero* I was with had abandoned me. I was depressed that day, and it was a Friday, around seven o'clock in the evening, and I'd taken some pills and I began thinking that the guy wasn't interested in me anymore, and he didn't even come to talk to me or chat with me, and I fell into such a weird depression that I decided to get a razor and cut myself. However, the other day, when I came out of the infirmary, I ran into him, and he said to me, "Hey, what happened?" and I said, "Well, I cut myself, and I hurt myself because you don't talk to me, or anything. You act like you don't care, you don't even speak to me anymore, and I decided to cut myself and so that day they sent me to the hospital." After that, the guy began talking to me again and we've been chatting and we've had sex, and he's the person I really love.

Interviewer: Are you in love with him?

Juan Carlos: Yes, of course.

Interviewer: Do you enjoy sex with him? When he penetrates you, does it feel good?

Juan Carlos: Sure it does.

Interviewer: Tell me a little about that.

Juan Carlos: I get satisfaction from the way the penis penetrates the anus and all those things. I get satisfaction on one hand, and he gets satisfied too. For me it's something very enjoyable.

Interviewer: I imagine that one of the things that a *cachero* needs to have is a big member, because if he has a small one, I imagine that he couldn't be a *cachero*. What do you say about that?

Juan Carlos: In my view, he has to be a normal person, not too exaggerated. But there are different tastes here. There are queens who are real happy with a "banana" [penis], hopefully one that's about two or more hands long.

Interviewer: And how about you?

Juan Carlos: Oh no, not me. The more medium-sized it is, the better. God forbid a big one! If one of those sons of bitches gets you, they split you open.

Interviewer: What else do you like? Tell me about kissing, about love.

Juan Carlos: Well, no, when you're going to have sex with someone you love, well, you embrace him, you kiss him as if he were a woman and when you have sex, that person pleases you, attracts you. It's something very exciting to have that relationship.

CHANGES IN SEXUAL PRACTICES

As with relationships between *cacheros* and transvestites, relationships between *cacheros* and *güilas* also undergo modifications. *Cacheros* tend to change roles, once a relationship is established. Luis tells us that he has seen cacheros in the bathroom performing fellatio on the *güilas*. Others allow themselves to be penetrated by the young men. "In my case, my partner asks us to change roles from time to time, so that we don't get bored. It's very natural," says Gerardo, a *güila*. Older *cacheros* tend to masturbate more because, as Carlos explains, "They can't get it up because of their age and so many drugs."

However, the most radical change is determined by the sudden end of youth. The *güilas* who arrive in jail are eighteen to twenty years old, and once they go beyond this age they cease to be such. "Being a *güila* lasts as long as a spring day," says Daniel. Before you know it, "the kids grow up, sprout hair and become men." Once this happens, the *cachero* must resume his search: "No, one cannot, and one does not want to go around with a *güila* who's beginning to look old, because it makes one seem like a gay," he continues.

For this reason, the *cacheros* themselves encourage their *güilas* to become *cacheros*. "Every *cachero* should know when to throw the chick out of the nest," Ernesto admits. "It's not easy, because you become fond of them and you don't want to lose them. However, it's necessary to do it, because sooner or later, they'll become men." Thus, the master must encourage his pupil to follow in his footsteps. "I don't want to see my *güila* turn into a queen or a gay. Never! I train him so that he himself will become a man and find another *güila* to treat like a woman. It's the law of the jungle."

Not all *cacheros* are as understanding or loving. Some even end up being murdered by the *güilas* themselves. "It is not all that unusual for *güilas* to take revenge against their former *cacheros*," says Juan Carlos. "One day I heard that a *cachero* had been killed precisely for having raped another *cachero* when he [the second] was a *güila*, he explains. "Another smashed his *cachero*'s face in and left him half dead," he adds. "The truth is, there's a lot of resentment because of the humiliations they've experienced." According to Daniel, "Many of the crimes against *cacheros* are committed by their former *güilas* who, when they became men, do not forget who raped them."

Chapter 4

Foxes

Relations between homosexual men that do not reflect gender or age differences—symbols of the masculine-feminine dichotomy—are not tolerated or respected in jail. However, these types of relationships do exist, though they are considered illicit. The men who practice them are known as *zorras* or foxes, people who hide or cover up their sexual activities.

Who are these foxes? There is no simple answer to this question. This group not only represents a marginal sector, but also an alternative discourse to *cacherismo*. There are many kinds of foxes: open gays and "in the closet" homosexuals, bisexuals, heterosexuals, and male prostitutes. We could say that foxes are as much a marginal group within the prison culture as they are an alternative sexual discourse. Foxes are symbols of a different model for homosexual relations. At the same time, they are the logical contradictions that arise from the impossibility of imposing a sexual model on the entire population. "We *zorras* are the ones who say, 'No, we're not going to follow the little game of *cacherismo*,'" says Marcos.

To clarify the phenomenon of *zorrismo*, it is best that the foxes themselves explain who they are and what they do. Marcos describes himself as a "legitimate *zorra*." "But what *is* a *zorra*?" we ask him. "A *zorra* is a man who likes men, or goes to bed with them without all this bullshit about 'active' and 'passive.'" To explain himself more clearly, he tells us his story:

> I'm a gay man. Before landing in jail for drugs, I led an open life in San José. I used to go to gay bars and I had affairs. For four years I had a relationship with two owners of a gay bar

who like threesomes. That pair of assholes were dealing coke, like me, but when I got busted they didn't do shit to help me. They abandoned me like a dog. They don't even dare to visit me, because they don't want to show their true colors, that pair of motherfuckers. Well, just imagine what it was like for me, who had never been in prison before, to end up among all this riff-raff. At first I was freaked out that the homosexuals in jail are the transvestites. Those horrible queens, all dressed up like women—they look more like lesbians than women. Well, you can imagine that I wasn't going to cook, wash, and iron for no shit *cachero*. When some son of a bitch would ask me why I didn't shave my legs and become a queen, I'd tell them to go shave their sisters' asses. For me, all those *cacheros* are really a bunch of frustrated queens who can't accept what they are. When they fuck around with me, I tell them, "You may be a *cachero* but you still give your ass like anyone else."

Marcos is a "modern" homosexual. He has a psychoanalytical perception of sexual orientation: people are defined by the object of sexual desire, not by what they practice. "A man who goes to bed with another man is gay," he says, "and don't give me that story that only the passive one is gay."

Bisexuals are considered another type of fox. José, for example, is a masculine man who had sexual relations with both men and women before going to jail. "I had a wife, but once in a while I enjoyed fucking a young boy," he tells us. José does not wish to be seen as a *cachero,* or as a homosexual, the only categories "allowed" in prison. "I'm interested in a relationship with a guy, but none of that crap about being a father or a husband, like a *cachero*, he says. "I don't think I should have to give money to anyone, just for fucking him, or be seen as a *cachero* who goes with *güilas*. I like to have a discreet fuck, and that's it. . . ." José is neither a *cachero* nor a homosexual, nor a *güila*, nor a transvestite. His relationships are discreet, though he himself admits that "I'm labeled a *zorra* and there's nothing I can do about it." However, he reveals that "I was as discreet as this before landing in jail. I'd never go to a gay bar, or hang out with queens. I have a wife and four kids."

Despite their great diversity, there are some common features in the relationships of *zorras*. One of these is that their relationships are not defined within the active-passive dichotomy. There are no clear rules about who should be active or passive in the sexual relationship. Their relationships are not based on differences in power or specialization regarding who penetrates whom. This includes both the "modern" gay relationship and prostitution. In neither case does one partner play the role of the man and the other the role of the woman.

Another common characteristic is that the inmates who are foxes are masculine. These individuals are considered foxes precisely because they can hide their homosexuality. The feminine homosexuals, whether transvestites or not, cannot pass for *zorras*; the *cacheros* will not allow them to. For this reason, only a minority of masculine homosexuals or bisexuals can be foxes.

Relationships between foxes are, in general, short-lived. Since *cacherismo* is the predominant sexual culture, inmates do not respect other types of couples. Foxes cannot allow themselves the luxury of having sex in the dens, in front of all their cellmates, and must do so furtively in the bathrooms, or when others are not around. It is not easy to maintain a relationship under these conditions. And because many foxes only engage in sex for money, they have no interest in establishing an emotional relationship.

To complicate matters further, foxes also have sexual relationships with *cacheros*, *güilas*, and other foxes. Julio, for example, is a fox. He is an attractive, masculine twenty-four-year-old. He is too old to be considered a *güila* but is sufficiently aggressive to command respect. "I've already sent more than one son of a bitch to the other side," he tells us proudly. However, from time to time, Julio enjoys "sodomy," as he calls it. Julio meets up with Vernon, a *cachero* of the old guard, in the bathrooms. "Vernon has a gay for a woman," says Julio, "I only want to have sex with him once in a while." Julio and Vernon have a passionate and totally macho relationship, as he describes it. "Vernon gets bored with that gay who's so feminine," he tells us. "I like rough macho sex. I think that men who go with women or gays are missing a real man's love." "What is man's love like?" we ask. "Well, it's the kind of love that doesn't make you feminine. Because when you only go with women or with gays, you become kind of effeminate with all that stuff about feelings and love and flowers and all that bullshit. Love between men is macho style: pain and pleasure and none of that sodomy."

Alberto is a fox who has sex with a *güila*. This relationship is completely secret, because "God forbid that the *cachero* should find out that I go with this kid!" he tells us fearfully. "Don't even think about mentioning names, 'cause I'll get pissed. Okay?" We asked him why he engaged in secret relationships instead of finding a *güila* for himself. Alberto explained: "No, I don't believe in relationships or in maintaining some kid. I go with this *güila* just for the hell of it. The kid's really gorgeous. Did you notice his ass? With those buns he could feed a whole bunch of us in this jail," he confesses.

Sometimes, *cacheros* have sex with each other. In this situation, the *cacheros* fall into the category of foxes, since they are stepping outside the rules of the game. Juan Carlos tells us that he has seen two *cacheros* having sex in the bathroom:

> I was about to take a shower one night, because it was so hot, when I found Pepe and Tomás, the husbands of Leticia and Sonia, in a real lather in the showers. I could hardly believe it, because if one of those queens finds out, all hell will break loose in the block! Sonia would really make a scene, because she tells the whole world that her husband is a real macho. Well, poor Sonia, because if she'd seen what I saw him doing, she'd fall on her ass.

Can a *güila* have sex with a transvestite? we asked Daniel. "Sure," he replies. "When a *güila* has sex with a transvestite, he's considered to be a little fox who escaped from the den." Daniel knows that some of the *güilas* who are "fed up being meat for the *cacheros*, seek their own satisfaction with the transvestites." Pedrito is one such example. He goes looking for Maripepa in the kitchen where she works, and, behind her husband's back, "I have her in the kitchen sink, with the lard that's used for cooking beans," he explains. "Who knows if the gallo pinto [typical dish of rice and beans] we eat contains the offspring of Pedrito and Maripepa," he tells us with a smile. "Is it possible for two *güilas* to have a relationship?" we ask Daniel. "That happens a lot. Look at Mario and

Ernesto. Both have their *cacheros*, but everyone knows they fuck each other behind their husbands' backs. Ernesto plays the macho with Mario, but with his *cachero* things are different," he replies.

Can a transvestite be a *cachero*? we ask Manuel, in some confusion. Manuel, a long-time *cachero* from the old Penitentiary replies without hesitation: "Yes, of course, Black Willy. That queen was feared because she was bad and because she was a witch. She knifed more than one person. Black Willy sometimes grabbed the young kids." According to Manuel, "Not all queens are passive. Willy was a man in bed, and he fucked more than one thug in jail. Nobody messed with her, and those who did wound up as stiffs." Pedro also has something to say on this point: "There are transvestites who have sex with each other. María Candelaria goes to bed with Penélope. I know it seems weird, but it's true. Many guys say they're both lesbians and they can't understand how two queens like them can make love. But, they're together and they're happy."

THE REVOLUTIONARY BACKSIDE

According to Foucault,[1] all human relationships are imbued with power. Both heterosexual and homosexual relationships are permeated by it. No human relationship, however simple it may be, is devoid of power. However, certain discourses are promoted to increase the dominion of some groups over others. Not all people have equal access to power, even less so if they are in prison, at the mercy of different degrees of physical force and aggressiveness. Some inmates are more powerful than others, which means that they impose their discourses and rules. The discourse of *cacherismo*, as we have seen, benefits the *cacheros*. It prevails because they wield control over the money and have the physical strength to subjugate the rest. The *cacheros* are not only the ones who penetrate the transvestites, but they are also the prison drug dealers and the main killers: in other words, the *coles* (gang bosses or tough guys). A *col* is an inmate who is feared for his capacity to kill, either directly or by using a hitman. In practice, the *col* "fucks" the entire jail: he uses some inmates as women, and others as followers, hitmen, and employees. Others are bought with favors and money. *Coles* control many things in prison: prostitution and the distribution of drugs, robberies, services, and information. They decide who gets attacked, who lives, and who dies.

The sexual discourse of *cacherismo* is theirs. On this basis, *coles* can continue as such, and at the same time can use other men as servants, either sexually or socially. But this situation does not go unchallenged. Those inmates who must submit to the control of the *cacheros* find ways of resisting them, because, as Foucault himself noted, "Ever since power has existed, there has been resistance."[2] In other words, sexual relations that do not conform to the rules and discourse of *cacherismo*, are ways of resisting, of not submitting to the power of the *coles*. From the transvestite who possesses a masculine inmate, to the *güila* who gives himself to a queen, the inmates sabotage the discourse of *cacherismo*. They demonstrate that sexual and social relations may be established in a different way, without a system in which some always give the orders and others obey. According to Rosa, a transvestite, "The act of my fucking a fox is my way of saying that I'm tired of being the passive one." In this context, the penis and the backside become weapons of subjection and of liberation. "This ass is revolutionary," says Clemente, a gay man. "It's the only thing I have to show that, just because they fuck me, it doesn't mean I'm a second-rate queen."

Similar actions, then, have different meanings. A *cachero* who allows himself to be penetrated by his transvestite lover shows that he is so macho and such a *col* that he can afford to "give his ass," as they say in prison slang. However, a transvestite who penetrates a *güila* sends another message: he says that power can be exchanged and that nobody should have a monopoly on it. For this reason, if *cacheros* discover such a transgression, someone will be punished. But if a *cachero* does the same, the rest of the inmates will simply "look the other way," as Maria Alejandra says. "*Cacheros* do what they like and nobody says a word. Some swallow more than the most voracious queen, but just you try to tell them that. . . ."

POWER AND SEX

Is a fox a revolutionary and a *cachero* an aggressor? There is no simple answer. If we consider the fact that a fox looks for more symmetrical relationships which are divorced from the power games of the *coles* and the *cacheros*, the answer would be a definite yes. However, foxes may also be seen as traitors: they introduce extraneous elements into the *cachero* culture, which are alien to the community of male inmates. Which, then, are the elements of what might be termed "prison colonialism"? The answer is very complex. "Foxes introduce a way of doing things that belongs to those pompous little gays from the city," Carlos, a traditional *cachero*, tells us. "And what's wrong with that?" we ask. "Well, it's the way of thinking of those goddamn cops and guards, who want to turn us guys into shit," he replies.

To understand what Carlos means, we need to pause along the way. We have said little about how judges, prison officers, social workers, psychologists, and others who work in the penal system influence prison culture. That is not the objective of this work and the task would require one or more books. However, it is important to take a brief look at the relations of power between prison officers and inmates.

Loss of freedom can be seen as a way of "feminizing" a man. From the time he is arrested, the inmate becomes dependent on others. If he wishes to make a phone call, get an appointment to see a doctor, change to another block or another bed, see a relative, cure a toothache, or play football, he must rely on the goodwill of others. I say goodwill, because prison officers "play" with their authority to make the prisoner more obedient and passive. Any prisoner who does not submit to their power is blacklisted, transferred to the most dangerous blocks, refused parole, locked up in a punishment cell, and even assassinated by a cell mate. Officers wield great power, which the prisoners must accept, "because if not, they fuck us all," says Carlos.

The inmates' submissiveness is almost theatrical: prisoners learn to address officers with great respect as "sir" or "ma'am," to produce a humble smile of gratitude when a favor is granted, to lower their eyes when an important visitor arrives, and to serve coffee and wash dishes when groups of Christians come to save their souls. "You have to oil the wheels with that bunch of motherfuckers, 'cause if you don't, they give you shit," says Luis. The submission is fake, but it hurts, "because you have to pretend to be good all the time, like you're in an election campaign," says María Fernanda, a transvestite.

Not only does the prisoner's behavior become feminized, but his life history is "colonized" or appropriated by psychologists, lawyers, and social workers. Mandatory therapy and participation in rehabilitation workshops mean that inmates are questioned by health professionals about their crimes. Unlike most inmates, these "experts" are from middle-class backgrounds and their psychoanalytical training makes them anticipate answers even before they ask the questions. Thus, in the course of their "therapies," they tend to look for what their training has taught them are the "causes" of criminal conduct: lack of love, broken homes, physical and emotional aggression, neglect, extreme poverty, and ignorance. The prisoners know very well what they must say to "soften up" those who will evaluate their aggression, or grant them parole. "María Emilia, the psychologist, nearly cries when I tell her that I became a transvestite because my dad raped me when I was a little kid," says Penélope. "I sniffle a little when I tell her that I prayed to God not to let my father hurt me, because he would leave me bleeding for days." "But did your story have an effect?" we ask. "Of course! María Emilia would say I was gay because of that aggression and that I could change if I wanted to. And that if I paid more attention to women and talked to them more, I would end up liking them." "And how did it benefit you to play along with her?" we ask. "Uh, well, in her report she would say that I was cooperating a lot and thinking about my life and she could see that I could change and be a good member of society. But, as soon as I left her office, I'd say to myself: "Oh, what a stupid bitch!" "And did you listen to the psychologist and pay more attention to women?" we asked. "Of course! I'd leave the office and turn to look at the secretaries and ask myself, 'Where did that creature buy those great heels?'"

Pedro José killed three men. We do not know why he killed them, nor did we ask him. However, he too knows what to say to obtain a more favorable evaluation that will get him out of maximum security. "Officials love to cloud the issue," he explains. "When they ask me about my crimes, I know what I need to say: I felt an enormous rage, I saw red, I didn't know what I was doing, and it was only when I opened my eyes that I realized my crime, which was the fault of that character of mine which I don't have now." Jonás does the same when prison officials review his case to decide whether he should be granted parole. "I just talk about my kids, that they don't have a dad and that I'm dying to see them. I tell them that they go to school and they hardly know me. That the youngest asks, 'Where's Daddy, where's Daddy?' That's the only way to make that bitch Nora, the social worker, feel sympathetic toward me, the great whore." "And does it work?" we ask. "Of course! With that story I always get permission." "Well, at least you get to see your kids," we reply. "Are you crazy? You know my whore of a wife got together with a butcher. I wouldn't go near those motherfuckers!"

Because communities of male prisoners are colonized, they establish mechanisms to resist oppression. These include alternative discourses, parallel power structures, social mobility, specific language, rituals, myths, and ceremonies. *Cacherismo*, for example, is a distinct discourse, independent from that which predominates in middle-class Costa Rican society. It is diametrically opposed to the religious discourse that condemns homosexuality. "I attend Christian services for the coffee and the empanadas they give us. But when they start preaching against sodomy, I turn a deaf ear, because those pious old broads don't know the great things they're missing," says Julio, a *cachero*. Emilio, another *cachero*, explains, "For me, sodomy is not an illness, as the unit psychologist says, but a natural way of satisfying yourself among men. I don't believe all that bullshit about the only way to make love is through the vagina."

In contrast to the Spanish used by the middle classes, the inmates have invented their own dialect. Where sexual terms are concerned, the words *cachero*, *zorra*, and *güila* substitute for the words "homosexual," "bisexual," and "heterosexual." This is more than a simple change. For the inmates, the world is divided into strong and weak, not into men and women. This reflects a different way of ordering things. Words that the middle classes use in one way are transformed into something else. A bisexual, according to the middle class, is a person who has sexual relations with men and with women. In prison slang, a bisexual is someone who is active and passive. This means that practice is more important than the object of sexual desire. To "modern" groups, the word gay means a homosexual who is aware of his or her sexual orientation and of belonging to the homosexual community. In prison, a "gay" is a transvestite. This means that not all those who have sex with men in an active way are homosexuals. The inmates, for their part, have their own initiation ceremonies, love rituals, gang rapes, and innumerable rules about what can and cannot be done, in the political, social, economic, and sexual arenas. One way of showing love, for example, is to slash one's wrists. When an inmate wishes to demonstrate his fidelity to another who does not return his affections, bloodletting is the way to do it. Another way is to tattoo the name of the transvestite or the *cachero* on the most intimate parts of the body. "I have Mono's name tattooed on my backside," confesses Endivia, a transvestite. "I had it done with the words 'Mono's Property.'" When two men marry, they cut their hands and exchange blood. "Now with AIDS, that practice is less common," says Pepe, "but it used to be a real marriage ceremony."

Cacheros, for their part, establish a parallel power inside the jail that rivals the power of the prison officers. The latter know they must respect the *cacheros* because otherwise things would become more difficult for them. *Cacheros* have the power to organize a strike or a riot, have a guard killed, buy favors, hire a hit man, maintain order, or create disorder," Daniel tells us. This power is wielded according to certain rational principles. Otherwise, the jail would be a permanent bloodbath. The fact that crimes are relatively few and far between, and that they have declined in recent years, means that the system is preserved through moderation. The *coles* impose their authority and run the prison's internal market in drugs, prostitution, and other services that are under their control. If there were no internal system of authority, chaos would prevail. "Look," says Puro, "this is a jungle. Unless order is imposed, nobody here respects anything. That's why it's important for people to learn who they shouldn't mess with and that there are things you can't do. We're like the internal law on the blocks, the guardians of prison morals."

The system imposed by the *coles* and the *cacheros* not only provides a certain security, but also a certain pride of belonging. Inmates aspire to be respected and feared like the *coles* and to enjoy some of their privileges. "Of course I feel proud to be a *col*," says Puro, "it's an honor that people respect me and ask for advice. I see that the rest look at me like a movie star and that when I speak, I'm respected." There is a system of promotion to reach the top. Nobody becomes a *col* as soon as he enters prison. A man must prove his masculinity, his independence from the authorities, his respect for other *coles*, his strength and, most important of all, his business skills and ability to subjugate his adversaries. This takes time and therefore the *coles* are generally the inmates who are serving longer sentences for more serious crimes.

What does this power structure have to do with the *cacheros* and the foxes? A lot. Every parallel system must protect the integrity of its institutions and ensure its independence from other power structures. *Cacherismo* establishes clear rules that differ from those outside prison. Thus, anyone who does not abide by these rules or who swears allegiance to other different models is attacked and persecuted. A "modern" homosexual who shares the official view that sexual orientation is determined by the object of desire and not by practice, as the *cacheros* believe, constitutes a danger to the system because he "introduces ideas that are alien to the jail," says Luis. An officer who is a fox and seeks sexual favors from inmates is a threat because, as Pacheco points out, "Sooner or later the inmate will open his mouth too much." A *güila* who questions the *coles'* control over the transvestites or a transvestite who does not respect their decisions will be the victims of assorted punishments, "because you have to respect the decisions of the elders," explains Polo.

It is for this reason that the prison community persecutes those who do not fit in with the *cachero* model: it senses that any changes call into question the most important structures in their daily lives.

Chapter 5

Relationships of Power and Money

Prostitution is common in prisons. In the questionnaire used during the holistic workshops of 1993, 81 percent of participants admitted that prostitution exists to some degree (see Table 5.1).

The most open form of prostitution occurs among transvestites. Although love relationships do develop between *cacheros* and transvestites and many remain faithful to each other for years, a majority of the latter end up working for *cacheros*. In spite of the great love professed by Toro or the indifference of Chino, many *cacheros* put their transvestite lovers to work. Prostitution is common in all prisons. Transvestite inmates are the ones who most frequently practice prostitution, since they have often done so before entering prison. When we asked a group of transvestites, in 1989, to state the number of sexual partners they had had, the interviewees reported an average of fifty-one during the previous twelve-month period (see Table 5.2).

One of the interviewees, a transvestite, had sex with 365 different partners. Given that there were 1,369 inmates at the time (excluding the forty-seven inmates in maximum security), this figure represents 27 percent of the prison's population. Five other transvestites had an average of 193 sexual partners during the same period. Since it is common for transvestites who prostitute themselves to have different clients, it may be deduced that a large number of inmates have sexual relations with them.

During the awareness course given to the transvestites, some interviewees who claimed not to have had any sexual partners in the questionnaire later admitted that they had indeed had up to five or even eight sexual contacts daily. When they were asked, during the course, about the number of different men they had had as sexual partners since their arrival in prison, eight of the interviewees gave figures that totaled 856—in other words, an average of 107, double the number they had indicated in the questionnaire.

TABLE 5.1. Aspects of Prostitution in Prison (in Percentages)

Variables	Pretest	Posttest
(N)	(188)	(188)
Total	100	100
How common is prostitution inside prison?		
Very common	18.1	14.9
Common	13.8	25.5
Regular	17.6	20.2
Not very common	22.3	21.3
Does not exist	25.5	17.0
No reply	2.7	1.1
Summary		
Does not exist	25.5	17.0
Exists to some degree	71.8	81.9
No reply	2.7	1.1

Source: Johnny Madrigal, *Impacto de la prevención del sida en privados de libertad costarricenses,* ILPES, San José, 1993.

TABLE 5.2. Number of Male Sexual Partners of Interviewees During Previous Twelve Months

Number of interviewees	Average number of sexual partners
2	0
4	1.5
6	5.5
5	22.8
5	193.8
Total 22	
Average	51
Median	7
Mode	–
Minimum	0
Maximum	365

Source: Jacobo Schifter and Johnny Madrigal, *Hombres que aman hombres,* ILEP-SIDA, San José, 1992, p.186

Note: The values 0, 1, 2, 4, and 6 sexual partners were each repeated twice.

The transvestite of the couple becomes the provider, an ironic situation in a relationship in which he plays the role of the woman. Some earn money by doing domestic chores for other inmates, such as washing and ironing clothes. Others organize raffles, selling numbers in combination with the National Lottery. However, in a penitentiary system that offers few opportunities, it is difficult for them to find suitable work. Nearly all of them consider the jobs to which they are assigned in industrial workshops or in the fields to be too arduous. Therefore, to satisfy their own needs and those of their partners, they turn to prostitution. This activity is concealed from their official lovers, for fear of reprisals.

In the prison sex trade, payment varies according to the client's resources. Charges range from small sums of money to doses of different drugs. There is great demand for sexual favors and there is stiff competition among the transvestites themselves, and between them and the foxes, who also charge for their services on occasion.

Cacheros often complain; "Now the foxes are everywhere and do anything for a hit of crack," as Luis says. The need for crack drives many men to prostitute themselves. Ever since crack began circulating in Costa Rican jails during the mid-1980s, prostitution has increased enormously. Many inmates are willing to perform oral or anal sex for just a few hundred colones. One allowed himself to be penetrated "for the eighty pesos [colones] I needed to buy crack." Some *cacheros* complain that they cannot stay faithful to their partners "because there are so many foxes who pursue us to fuck them for money," says Mario. Pedro says he cannot take a shower in peace, because "as soon as I take my clothes off, there are three or four kids looking for me to fuck them." Gerardo confirms this: "I think they've set up a breeding zoo for foxes. I'd never seen so many before. Sometimes I can't believe that there are so many macho men who'll do anything just to buy crack."

Competition in prison, as in any capitalist market, drives prices down. Where a prostitute might once have been able to charge 2,000 colones, prices have now dropped to 200 colones. The supply is plentiful, according to prostitutes and clients. "Hell! The situation is terrible now," a prostitute tells us. "Before we had the luxury of choosing our clients. Now you can't do that. Any crack head is willing to give his ass for a joint." This is Juan Alberto's view of the situation:

> Yeah, the *cacheros* spread the money around . . . maybe they take a shine to more than one kid who's into sodomy. They have sex with one and then with another. Most of the people here are forty or fifty years old and as they're on their own and don't get conjugal visits or anything, then they pay several kids. There are about three kids here who are into having affairs with different men, you see. Maybe to earn three or four hundred colones, I don't know what for, most of these kids go with the *cacheros*, the men with the money, who pay them. They whore at night or during the day, but they're not together. When they need money, they go to a *cachero* so that he'll make love to them and pay them. There's a kid here who goes with several at the same time, so that they'll fuck him and have sex with him for money, mainly because of his crack addiction."

Ana Rosa is a transvestite who prostitutes herself. When she lived in San José's red-light district, she dealt drugs and was involved in prostitution. In jail, she has continued with both occupations. The inmates assume that Ana Rosa will automatically be available to anyone who pays. Zorro talks about his relationship with her:

> When I saw that queen, Ana Rosa, walk into the block, I just drooled. She looked so feminine and pretty that it was almost impossible to believe she was a man. She changed pants in her cell and I saw that pert, firm little ass of hers. I noticed that I wasn't the only one looking at her. Several guys in my block were saying to her, "Hey, honey, little turkey butt," and she pretended not to pay attention. I called one of them over, and made a real face at him and told him, "You better lay off that queen and leave her to me until I get bored with her." The guy didn't like what I said, but he left and told the others. I walked over to that queen and told her, "Hey, honey, you'd better sleep with me at night, 'cause if you don't, they might do something bad to you tonight. Sleep in my bed and I'll take care of that little treasure you have there." She smiled at me and I saw that

she liked me. I know that gays like me because they say I'm good-looking and well-endowed. But then she said she needed money and that she charges a toucan [five thousand colones] for her "little treasure." "Don't be so dumb," I told her. "If you don't sleep with me tonight, that gang that was flirting with you is gonna give you such a surprise that tomorrow you won't be able to walk." She wasn't dumb and she came to sleep with me that night. I told her, "You're gonna eat all of this and for free, you hear that, honey? And I'm only gonna pay you with milk [semen]." For three nights I had her all to myself in my den. Ana Rosa howled like a bitch, probably to get everyone all stirred up. Then I let her charge other people, so long as she paid me a toucan for protection.

Ana Rosa admits that even when she falls in love and wants to be faithful to one man, her cell mates will not let her:

I began to like this blond kid who's in my block. He's very macho but young. He has a face like an angel and a very beautiful smile. He began to flirt with me and we would talk together in the afternoons when the others were playing football. Once he kissed me passionately and touched my breasts. I take hormones so I have big ones. He took off my blouse and began to suck them, but very delicately. Then he led me to the bathroom and took off all my clothes and began to rub soap all over me. He took off his clothes too and he had a beautiful body. He was totally excited and began to make love to me. It was really wonderful, extremely passionate, and when he possessed me, he said, "This belongs only to me, you understand? I don't want anybody else coming in here." But he was only twenty years old and real green. For a few days I was his. We would make love like crazy in his bed. I was so in love that I didn't want to take any clients so that I wouldn't make him suffer. But they didn't let me. One night, Zorro and two of his friends dragged us out of bed. They grabbed him and beat the shit out of him. Then they dragged me by the hair to the bathroom and brutally raped me. The kid was moved to another block and I had to stay with all these sons of bitches. After that, I preferred to keep charging and paying Zorro to protect me. In here you have no choice.

Other transvestites resort to tricks to avoid splitting their profits with others. Permanent Halloween (so-called because she is "frighteningly" ugly) told us how she managed to set up her own business:

> I've always whored in the red light district. There I learned to use a knife on any son of a bitch who tries to screw with me. Once, I charged a *cachero* called Ingeniero a thousand colones for a fuck. After we finished he didn't want to pay up, and he said, "Honey, you're too flaccid you ain't worth it." The idiot didn't want to pay me. "Look here, you mangy scab, before you were telling me how delicious I was and now you say you're not paying me." So, I grabbed a knife and split his face open. He tried to kill me, but he couldn't. I'm stronger than an ox. They took him to the infirmary and put about ten stitches in him. I was sent to a punishment cell and then to medium security. But when I got there I said, "Anyone who wants to fuck me shows me the money first, or else." I'm not going to work for any son of a bitch who doesn't give his ass honestly like I do.

As far as prostitutes are concerned, it comes as no surprise that the guards or prison officers also require their services:

> Colonel W. likes transvestites. Sometimes he invites Casandra and me to the office, supposedly to sort out a matter in our files. He pays us 500 colones to suck him off together.

Despite the fact that inmates prefer sex as a business, they are also victims of a powerful compulsion which leads them to regard sexual relations as a means of satisfying other psychological needs, something that aggravates their situation. This fact is borne out by various responses given on sexual issues.[1] Many inmates (45 percent) agree that sex is the only way to relax in moments of tension, and 36 percent believe that when they feel insecure, the best thing to do is to find a new sexual partner. Another 41 percent think about sex continuously.

PROSTITUTION AMONG FOXES

Some men have sex only for money. They do not feel any attraction to other men, as in the two cases mentioned above. Juan Alberto is an example of a fox who charges, even though he does so furtively. He admits that since he took up prostitution, "I don't have a need for things because I can easily afford them." Horacio is married and has conjugal visits with his wife. He is also extremely masculine and is never seen with homosexuals or transvestites. However, his addiction to crack is enormous. When his friends in the block are asleep, says José, Horacio hires himself out for money:

> I really couldn't believe it. That guy is very masculine and a great football player. But since he's been into crack, his personality's changed. One night I needed to pee, so I went to the bathroom about two-thirty in the morning and found him with another guy—I prefer not to give his name. Horacio was nailed down like a common whore. I pretended not to see anything and went back to bed. After a few minutes, he came to warn me not to say anything, because he just needed the money. Well, I've seen him going to the bathroom several times. Here everyone pretends that nothing is happening.

Another fox who sells his favors is Carrasco, a gay man. His business is to offer oral sex for 300 colones. Carrasco has a number of clients whom he visits in the afternoon and at night. He says he sometimes earns as much as 4,000 colones a day:

> I've always enjoyed giving head. All my life I've enjoyed taking young kids and giving them a good session of oral sex. But in jail, I do it for money, to buy marijuana and better food. I go to different clients and sometimes I drink the milk [semen] of about twenty or thirty guys a day. That's why they call me Pinito [a brand of milk]. It doesn't bother me to be called that. What I can't stand is those whores of transvestites who make fun of me and say I'm dirty and call me names like Chupacabras [Goat Sucker] to humiliate me.

Inmates are not the only foxes. In one jail there is a toilet which is used by visitors, prison officers, and inmates. Roberto describes what he saw one day:

> I had terrible diarrhea that day, so I went into the toilet that is just outside the blocks. I was about to go in when I saw an officer coming out with Xavier, the *cachero* who goes with La Niña. The cop was a young kid, good-looking. When they saw me they acted kind of strange. I noticed that Pedro, another friend of Xavier, was acting like a look-out. It seemed very strange, but I didn't think anything of it. A few days later, I heard them calling Xavier to go to the office for something. I happened to notice that instead of going to the office, he went to the bathroom again. Once again, Pedro went with him. The cop went in and they were in there for about twenty minutes. I told my friend Ernesto about what I'd seen and he said that Xavier was doing it with the kid. "With the cop?" I asked. "Yeah," he said, "Xavier likes sodomy and he pays the policeman to give it to him. Don't you see, the guy has money from drugs and the cop's into crack too."

There are some foxes in high places, as Vernon recounts:

> I like queens, I don't deny it. But real queens. The more they look like women, the better I like them. I'm not turned on by the fox types. I'd heard that this guy liked inmates to fuck him. I also knew that he'd asked about me a few times. I'm blond and that guy would always be looking at me kind of strange. But he was a real son of a bitch and he'd already refused me a fifty-five [a type of parole]. When he called me in, I don't know what for, I felt him looking at me very strangely. After a few minutes of talking bullshit about my case, he asked me if I'd like to have a drink in his office. I said yes, but not today because I was very tired after working in the fields. I said that I'd accept a drink, but for two reds [2,000 colones]. He said sure, and asked when I'd like to come. I said next week. Well, that shitface never imagined that he couldn't treat me like a

whore. I decided to report him to a female prison officer. She said she'd talk to someone else and told me to go ahead with the meeting so they could catch him red-handed. Well, the following week I went in and he gave me a drink and invited me to dance. Then he asked if he could kiss me. I told him I was scared because someone might see us, but he said no, that the guards were patrolling and that there was nobody except us two and a guard who didn't know what was happening. I had trouble getting an erection, but I made it and I began to fuck him when Doña Tulia walked in and caught us in the act. That son of a bitch still doesn't know that I set him up.

RAPE

The issue of rape, known as "attacks," is confidential in prison. This means that inmates are exposed to great danger if they admit the existence of rape to strangers. In our case, we were able to discuss this issue only after years of working with the inmates. In the course of our first inquiries, the common response was that rapes did not occur. However, with the passing of the years, we gradually obtained different information from the inmates. Of the inmates who participated in the holistic workshops in 1993, 65 percent admitted that rapes occur. The difference in the questionnaires distributed at the beginning and end of the eight-week workshop show that more inmates are willing to admit that rape exists when they get to know us better (42 percent deny the existence of rape at the beginning of the workshop and only 33 percent do so at the end) (see Table 5.3).

The interviewees described the problem of rape, which may occur when a person first enters prison or later, and may involve the participation of several inmates. The victim is usually threatened with a knife and rendered defenseless by his attackers. In these brutal attacks, condoms are obviously not used, which makes these incidents a very dangerous source of possible AIDS infection. Because the jails are so overcrowded, cell blocks have become areas of great danger, to the point where the prison officers do not dare to enter every day. They do so only during periodic searches, when the number of guards is increased.

TABLE 5.3. Aspects of Rape in Prison (in Percentages)

Variables	Pretest	Posttest
(N)	(188)	(188)
Total	100	100
How common are rapes in this prison?		
Very common	5.9	6.4
Common	6.4	8.0
Medium	12.8	8.0
Not very common	30.3	31.4
Do not occur	42.6	33.5
No answer	2.1	1.6
Summary		
Do not occur	42.6	33.5
Occur to some degree	55.4	64.9
No answer	2.1	1.6

Source: Jacobo Schifter and Johnny Madrigal, *Hombres que aman hombres,* ILEP-SIDA, San José, Costa Rica, 1992.

The dormitories and toilets are a no-man's-land, dominated by gangs headed by the most dangerous prisoners. These gangs make the rules and run life in the jail, including the sex trade. They are also the ones who order rapes.

The motives for these attacks are varied. Sometimes they occur during a transvestite's first days in prison, before he has found the protection of a "godfather" who is respected by other inmates. His rape, then, has two meanings: it gives the *cacheros* power to exploit the transvestite and to decide who can and cannot pass for a fox. An example of this was the rape of Lulu, a twenty-three-year-old transvestite who was jailed for dealing marijuana. She had worked as a waiter in Alajuela and occasionally prostituted herself. She was a slender and effeminate transvestite. When she arrived in prison, instead of seeking the protection of a *cachero*, she teamed up with a young man with whom she established a relationship. This man was masculine but very young—only twenty-two. Lulu had sex with him and they decided to become a couple. This was not acceptable to the *cacheros* on the block. "That little queen ain't going to tell us who's a *cachero* around here," explained Pepe, one of the block's *cacheros* and *coles*. To "teach" him "who is who" in this block, Pepe summoned four of his cronies and one night:

> I was sleeping with my lover when I felt a knife at my neck. They told Gerardo, my partner, to keep still and that he'd better not see or hear anything. I begged Pepe not to do anything to me and to leave Gerardo alone. But it didn't work. Loro, another *cachero*, put his hand over my mouth and, between the four of them, they dragged me to the bathroom. I screamed whenever I could, but nobody paid any attention. As he pushed me into the bathroom, Pepe punched me in the mouth and made me bleed. I begged him to leave me alone, not to rape me because I'd do whatever they wanted. But it was too late. They ripped my pants and stripped me. They pulled their pants off and grabbed my legs and forced them apart. Pepe decided to abuse me first, without any lubricant, or saliva or anything. The pain was terrible. I couldn't feel anything except the pain and my blood flowing. Then the other three followed. It all lasted maybe twenty minutes, but for me it was an eternity. When they finished they slashed one of my buttocks with the knife and warned me: "If you talk, you big whore, we'll kill you tomorrow. Every time you take a shit, you'll remember this." I went back to my bed and a queen, Zancuda, bandaged my wound and gave me a tranquillizer to calm me down. I was crying hysterically.

Edwin was also raped soon after he arrived in prison. He was just eighteen, the golden age of the *güilas*. He is fair-skinned with pleasant features, brown hair, and a well-proportioned body. Edwin is a very masculine juvenile offender. His specialty was breaking into cars until he was arrested in a police raid. When he entered prison, he did not have the slightest interest in homosexuality and he rejected Julio, a forty-three-year-old *cachero* who made advances to him:

> I told him I didn't want any sodomy, that I wasn't into it. He said okay, that we could be friends, and he stopped bothering me. Little by little, he began to give me sleeping pills, to make

my time in prison go faster. One Saturday, around five in the afternoon, I was very drowsy on pills and he came to my bed and took out a knife and said, "Okay, now take your pants down and don't make any noise because I'll kill you right now." I tried to get away, but the son of a bitch had me by the waist and was pulling me back. No matter how hard I tried to cut loose, that bastard was too strong for me. When he was inside me, he said, "You ain't no little gentleman anymore; you're being conquered and now everyone knows it. Nobody respects a *güila* who's been possessed. Tomorrow you'll be pursued by another, and the day after tomorrow by yet another. You either submit to me, or you'll see what they'll do to you." I felt a terrible humiliation. Then I noticed that two friends of his had come to see what was going on and they were laughing at me.

It often happens that a transvestite rejects the sexual advances of a particular inmate, which leads to his being raped by the one who was rejected and others who conspire with him. When a transvestite who has joined a particular gang, and gained its protection in exchange for sex or money, decides to join another gang, retribution is also swift: gang rape is the price of desertion. A transvestite who displays very refined, "high class" manners is also a candidate for rape, to teach him that this kind of behavior is not acceptable in jail. Infidelity between couples is also punished in the same way. The wronged lover joins with the rest of the gang in attacking the traitor.

Rape is also used as a form of revenge against nontransvestite inmates. When a fox charges for his services without giving the *cacheros* a cut of his earnings and competes with the transvestites, the "owners" of the latter conspire either to turn the fox into a transvestite or force him out of the business.

Like I told you, I'm not a transvestite and never was. I liked to give oral sex for money to some guys, something exclusive, not with anyone. But I didn't like to go with *cacheros* or shave myself or go around like a whore or wash anyone's clothes. Well, one night Mono's gang grabbed me and raped me. There were five guys. They said, "Hey, shit-fox, if you keep on sucking and charging for it, we're gonna cut off your dick and dress you up like a queen."

The attacks occur at night in the cells and the toilets. Victims who resist get hurt. Afterward, the victim never reveals the names of his aggressors, because the price for doing so is death. Recovery from the trauma suffered takes place without any member of the prison's health or security staff being aware of the incident.

When one man—or several—rape another, does this constitute a sexual relationship or is it yet another form of violence? The answer, according to Tejón, is not simple. He admits having participated in more than one of these incidents. The reasons for the attacks have already been examined. However, we asked him how he managed to get an erection given that, to commit rape, there must be desire. "Of course," he answered, "you get excited when you have control over a person." According to Tejón, all sexual relationships are based on power and it is this which excites men:

> If you want to know how you can get an erection, even when you don't like men, I'll tell you a story. As you can see, I'm a guy. Women like me. I don't need to force any woman to possess her. But I'm a macho; I like difficult things. Men are born hunters. We like to possess, the way any beast attacks another. All that stuff about men and women making love is for idiots. What we want to do is dominate, penetrate a woman so that she knows who's boss. I'm here because I raped a fifteen-year-old girl. But it wasn't fair because that little bitch wanted a dick. Well, she was my cousin and came to live with us because her family moved to the United States. One afternoon I found her naked with her boyfriend in her room. He wanted to have her but she said no, she wanted to be a virgin when she gets married. Although the guy kept insisting, she persuaded him that they should just masturbate each other. My cousin was a real little fox and she was protecting her little pussy like it was gold! Well, the following week I waited 'til she was alone in her room and I suddenly walked in. I kissed her on the mouth. I knew she liked me because I noticed that she didn't resist. I'd noticed her flirting with me before. I took her clothes off gently and then her bra. She came out with the same line about not

wanting to be penetrated, that we should just play around and nothing more. I said yeah, sure, that I respected her like a young lady. But, when she least expected it, I told her the truth: "You're gonna be mine!" She began to try to get out of the bed, but I grabbed her hard. I began slapping her face to scare her. When I saw her crying and begging me not to rape her, I got even more turned on. The sweat, the tears, the begging, and the screams are all part of the excitement. I would touch her with the tip [of the penis] and hold still. The more I did it, the more she believed that I wouldn't possess her, that I was sorry. But no. After half an hour of playing around I broke through and made her mine. I'm telling you this because you feel the same thing with a guy. When Castillo was raped, I felt the same. The guy deserved punishment. When he saw that we were going to get him, he begged us not to rape him, he said he wouldn't steal our drug money again. The idiot was sweating and crying and begging for mercy. No mercy and no shit! We took off his clothes and waited a few minutes to let him beg and plead with us not to do anything. When he thought we'd forgiven him, Gavilan took off his clothes and told us to lay him on his back and spread his legs open. When Gavilan got on top, the screams of pain made us all crazy. Castillo was raped without mercy.

Tejón does not believe that sexuality inside jail is any different from sexuality outside. He believes that all men, deep down, are potential rapists. "That line that says men are made to be faithful is a priest's tale. They're the ones who know the least about sex," he tells us. Tejón believes that males are predators by nature.

Men are born hunters. We like challenges. There's nothing more boring than having sex with your wife, the one you can have every day. After a few months, you're fucking her but thinking about other women. Soon, you need to have an affair. There's nothing more delicious for a man than to dominate a woman who resists. You want a fight, a struggle. Can't you see that the penis is a knife? Few women want us to put the whole of this cock inside them. You have to persuade them, trick them, promise them everything, so they'll let you. Well, that's what males like and it doesn't matter if you stick your dick into a broad or a guy.

Although it seems extreme, Tejón is not completely wrong. We do not yet know how important power is as a source of sexual attraction. Sometimes we believe that what attracts us about a person is his or her body. However, we do not believe that the sexual organs are attractive in themselves. They become interesting when we imbue them with power and resistance. They are desirable for what they signify and not for the way they look. When the bodies of men and women are imbued with meanings of power and resistance, there are possibilities for altering the typical relationship. In this way, the bodies of men may be redefined as feminine and those of women as masculine.

Though cruel and extreme, prison rapes follow certain precepts and do not occur every day. As we have seen, they contain a combination of erotic and political aspects. Prisoners who have participated in rapes regard them as a ritual similar to the possession of any victim, whether male or female.

One of the objectives is to prevent other discourses and inmates from challenging the rules of the *cacheros*. If a prisoner rebels against the accepted system of homosexuality, in which *cacheros* dominate and exploit others, he will be attacked. Thus, the transvestites or *güilas* who do not accept their condition or do not wish to seek the protection of one man will be raped "so that they find a godfather," as Juan Carlos says. Another objective of rape is to prevent other models of homosexuality from establishing themselves as legitimate. For this reason, attacks are sometimes perpetrated against "modern" gay couples or against a fox who crosses the accepted boundaries and becomes too obvious. The message is that these relationships are not respected and must remain clandestine. An additional objective of the rapes is to sexually initiate heterosexual prisoners and decide who fits into each category. A young man cannot aspire to be a *cachero* and if he attempts to be one, he will be raped. The same will happen to a very effeminate man who tries to break free from a partnership or from prostitution.

Other nonsexual functions of rape are to punish inmates who are informants, who talk too much, who steal from the *coles*, who do not pay their debts, who flirt with other men's wives or girlfriends, who do not obey orders, and all who rebel against the power of the *coles* and the *cacheros*.

One additional function of rape is as a "punishment of the people." It is understood that certain crimes are unacceptable to prison society and deserve the worst punishment. One of these is child rape. Inmates who have raped children are themselves likely to be the victims of such attacks. "We might be criminals but we have certain principles," says Pico de Lora. "One of these principles is that children are innocent and must not be touched." The "people's punishment" is also meted out to those who steal from the poor. "Here we're waiting for that son of a bitch who stole millions from the people's bank so that he'll feel what it's like to be fucked the way he fucked all of us," adds Pico de Lora.

Chapter 6

Risk Factors in Sexual Relationships

A number of factors place the prison population at risk of contracting the HIV virus. However, homosexuality per se is not one of them. Each one of the sexual contacts described earlier may take place in a safe or an unsafe manner. A 1989 study on infection risk among transvestites identified several factors that facilitate the spread of the AIDS virus. It is important to consider their impact on sexual relations among inmates.

ALCOHOLISM AND DRUG ADDICTION

There is a high rate of drug consumption in prison. Despite rigorous controls, cocaine, marijuana, and barbiturates are readily available and are consumed daily. It is common for inmates to prepare *chicha*, an alcoholic drink made by fermenting any grain or food. Using containers which they have previously hidden, the inmates pour in water and then food (such as bread) and allow it to ferment. Sometimes they add discarded batteries. A few days later they drink the liquid that results from this mixture. The large amounts of drugs and *chicha* that are consumed daily constitute a major risk factor in the transmission of AIDS.

This risk begins with the way in which drugs are introduced into the prison. During Sunday visits, women bring drug-filled condoms, hidden in their vaginas, through the prison gates. There, a transvestite will introduce a condom, carried by one of the women, into his rectum. This maneuver, conducted very hurriedly, clearly constitutes a major risk of infection. "Some transvestites are chosen for this difficult mission because of the ample size of their backsides," says Pico de Lora. "La Carrasqueri is the favorite one because she has the biggest backside. She can put up to a pound of coke up her ass."

In the study on transvestites, the group admitted using marijuana before having sex. Of those who smoke, 42 percent said they used it always or nearly always before sex. Many inmates (59 percent) had also tried cocaine.[1]

To continue the analysis of the link between drugs and unsafe sex, the study found that cocaine use is related to the practice of active and passive anal penetration without the use of a condom. Moreover, a significant link was found between liquor consumption and passive sexual relations. This is corroborated by the fact that 42 percent of the group interviewed admitted that taking alcohol or drugs had influenced their decision on condom use.[2]

The same result was obtained through the questions that referred to the respondents' sense of self-control. Here, 55 percent agreed that they had problems with safe sex when they were intoxicated.

These findings confirm the results of similar studies conducted by Stall[3] and others, by Bye[4] among homosexuals in San Francisco,[4] and Connell in Australia.[5] Baumann and others, in a study of 160 gay men in New York, found that the combination of drugs and sexual activity was the most important factor in predicting a seropositive condition.[6] Prieur, in an ethnographic study in Oslo, found that men who became intoxicated prior to a sexual encounter tended to practice unprotected anal intercourse.[7]

Drugs are a part of prison culture. They are intimately related to the problem of time. When a person is in jail and the sentence is long, the only consolation is intoxication. It serves not only as an escape from reality, but as something else to which little attention has been paid: time control. An inmate lacks power over the most basic aspects of his life: he cannot decide where or when to eat, sleep, exercise, relax, receive visits, or see a doctor. But he can, thanks to drugs, play with time. A good dose of cocaine or lorazepam can make a week seem like a day. A tranquilizer taken with *chicha* makes the months seem shorter. A snort of crack increases the sense of well-being and reduces the waiting. When drugs are combined with sex, the pleasure extends beyond the few seconds that an orgasm lasts. "When I rub cocaine on my penis," says Toro, "I can go for hours before coming. The orgasm seems to last forever. When I finally come, I feel days have gone by since I got into the bed." Certain days are not even felt because the inmates are completely asleep.

Drugs reduce the inmates' reasoning capacity. It is not surprising that they should wish to forget their daily woes and miseries. "Who wants to think about life when you're stuck in this shit hole?" says Pico de Lora. But forgetting has its price. And prevention is one of the things that people forget about when they are intoxicated.

CONDOM USE AND ATTITUDES TOWARD CONDOMS

In his study on condom use, Bye found that negative attitudes toward condom use are related to unsafe sexual practices.[8] In work groups with gay American men, it was found that those who enjoyed unprotected anal sex had negative attitudes toward condom use. In Australia, Connell and others observed that positive attitudes toward condom use were related to the practice of safe sex.[9]

A 1989 study of homosexuals in La Reforma found that a low percentage of inmates always used a condom, while nearly three-quarters of those studied had been penetrated without a condom during the previous thirty-day period.[10]

This means that inmates in that particular prison constitute a group which has reservations about condom use, and 73 percent said they felt condoms reduce sexual pleasure.

A study of the inmates who participated in the AIDS-prevention workshops of 1993 reveals that the situation had improved. Of the 188 inmates who completed the questionnaire, the percentage who said they "never" used a condom decreased from 51 percent in the pretest questionnaire to 36 percent in the posttest. However, nearly four out of every ten inmates said they "never" use a condom, and another 22 percent "almost never" do. Only 12 percent said they use a condom "almost always," and 35 percent believe that "When you love your partner, you stop using a condom." Only 19 percent said they found it pleasurable to use a condom.

"Toro, why do you think that it's hard for inmates to use a condom?" we asked. "Because it doesn't feel the same. Here in jail, we want to have contact with flesh. We want to feel the juices, the milk [semen] like a sign of power. I personally like Angelita to feel my warm milk up her ass. It's like I'm fertilizing her." Toro believes that prisoners' bodies are so repressed that ejaculating freely is one of the few freedoms they have. "Think about it, you're in jail and you can't get out. The condom is like another jail that imprisons the semen. It traps it, tricks it, grabs it, and kills it. You want your dick to be free of constraints and limitations." We ask Toro about prevention. "Don't prisoners worry about being infected with AIDS and dying from it?" "Sure," he replies, "But that's just one of the many dangers you face in jail and maybe not the most immediate. Here you can die from many things worse than AIDS."

INTIMACY

The type of relationship in which an inmate is involved is important. From this, it is possible to deduce that condom use among transvestites and open homosexuals depends on the decision of their clients and lovers. Despite this situation, in a group with such well-defined patterns as prison inmates, a hierarchy is clearly established, especially in relation to the dominance exercised by the *cachero* over the transvestite, who is constantly under threat. An outburst of jealousy can easily turn into a knife fight. Nearly all the transvestites are marked by scars, evidence of fights with their partners. In assuming the role of the woman in the couple, they are trapped by the obligations and the virtual absence of rights experienced by women in Latin American societies. Even though both are aware of the effectiveness of condoms in the prevention of sexually transmitted diseases, the *cachero* refuses to use one. This is evident in the closed types of relationships between *cacheros* and transvestites, where unsafe sex is most frequently practiced. For example, in this type of relationship, an average of 10.7 anal penetrations occur each month, without the protection of a condom, while in a more open relationship, the monthly average is 4.3. In this last case, the practice of anal penetration with a condom is minimal, while in a closed relationships it is not used at all (see Table 6.1).

TABLE 6.1. Average Active and Passive Anal Penetrations Without Condom Use in Past Thirty Days According to Type of Relationship

	Average Anal Penetrations					
	With Ejaculation		Without Condom		With Condom	
Type of Relationship	A*	P*	A	P	A	P
Number interviewed	(22)	(22)	(22)	(22)	(22)	(22)
Average penetrations	0.4	7.1	0.8	5.4	0.04	1.3
Type of relationship						
Closed	1.0	14.9	2.1	10.7	0.0	2.6
Open	0.2	4.7	0.3	4.3	0.09	0.9
Celibate	0.0	0.0	0.0	0.0	0.0	0.0
(Eta* 100)	49	66	59	55	21	35

Source: Jacobo Schifter and Johnny Madrigal, *Hombres que aman hombres,* ILEP-SIDA, San José, Costa Rica, 1992, p. 193.

* Refers to active and passive penetration

In the AIDS-awareness training course, transvestites said they found major problems in trying to convince *cacheros* to use a condom when practicing anal sex. The very suggestion arouses the latter's suspicions about their partners' faithfulness. The transvestite's lack of power, given his role in the relationship, makes it difficult to get this concession. This is evident if we see that among other factors that influence the decision on condom use, 58 percent of the interviewees said their partner's attitude was the determining factor.[11]

When asked if the AIDS-prevention workshops had helped them in any way, their answer was a definite yes. They said they had received information on how to protect themselves from infection, and this had helped to improve their relationships with partners, girlfriends, wives, and family members. A typical response came from Juan Alberto:

Interviewer: How did you find out about AIDS?

Juan Alberto: Through the holistic course I took in San Sebastián, given by Don Tomás [a facilitator] and your team of co-facilitators. That's how I found out about it, how I heard about AIDS. Before that workshop, I was green and didn't know what it was. I'd heard comments, that you could catch it through a sexual relationship with a man or a woman, but mostly between homosexuals, and that's how the AIDS virus developed. And thanks to that course I did with you and other cofacilitators, I heard that anyone could infect you and I got an idea of what it is and how to prevent that disease.

Interviewer: How do you prevent it?

Juan Alberto: Well, by using condoms and also by taking care when you get a tattoo. You shouldn't get stuck with a needle that isn't new, because someone can pass the virus on to you that way—it's also transmitted that way.

Interviewer: Do you like using a condom, or not?

Juan Alberto: Well, let's say there are people who don't feel the same about condoms, right, but for me prevention is better, so I prefer to use a condom.

Interviewer: Do you insist that the *cachero* use a condom?

Juan Alberto: Sure! I always take a condom and give it to him. Otherwise I won't do anything with him.

Interviewer: Have you seen people using condoms in here?

Juan Alberto: Here there's just a few, but in San Sebastián nearly the majority of us who were in there used condoms. Rojas, our group facilitator, would start to tell the gays and the *cacheros* about that, to take care, to ask for condoms and all those things, and most of us used them.

In addition, some recognize that the discussion of drugs has prompted them to seek help to give up their drug habits.

Interviewer: Tell me a little about your relationship with drugs.

Juan Alberto: When I was in the other jail, I was heavily into crack and all that, but in here I've been keeping away from it.

I smoke marijuana and I'm getting into pills. But I've felt a little freer from crack, because at the other place I was heavily into that vice and now, thank God, I've been keeping away from it and avoiding it. Only, from time to time I smoke my [marijuana] joints.

Interviewer: Did you take the ILPES antidrugs workshop?

Juan Alberto: Sure.

Interviewer: Did it help you at all?

Juan Alberto: Yeah, the workshop helped me a lot in giving up crack and [explaining] what drug addiction is. However, through that [course] I was able to give up crack, which was the worst problem I had. And now, like I say, I'm doing okay, because I still have a joint [of marijuana] and now I'm getting into pills.

Interviewer: But you gave up crack?

Juan Alberto: Sure I did! I haven't smoked crack again. Only when I'm here and I get the urge I smoke a joint, but it's not all the time.

However, when asked about condom use, many inmates give a different answer: they use condoms in casual sexual encounters, but do not use them with their regular or permanent partners. Martínez believes his partner is faithful to him and will not betray him. Toro is certain that Angelita makes love "only with me," and moreover, he says, "I don't like condoms." When we ask him how he can be so sure, he replies, "I knew her without AIDS and we've had tests done and we're fine. We do them [the tests] every three months, and if one of us turns out to be infected, there would have to be a reason, and we would know that there had been infidelity." Daniel believes that since "my partner is faithful," he only needs to use the condom "from time to time." When we asked him if he found the workshop useful, he replied, "The workshop was very useful. I've seen many *cacheros* who use condoms, really, but in my case, I don't feel it's necessary because if this *güila* is unfaithful to me, he knows I'll kill him." The inmates feel it is important for them to take certain risks through the promises they make to each other. Their lives are not without danger, so it is hardly surprising that their relationships should include danger. Removing the risk from a relationship is something that, apparently, they do not wish to do. Although we may consider this position illogical, it is not entirely irrational. For example, in Angelita's case, she knows that if she infects her man, she will be stabbed to death. Perhaps this threat is not as effective as a condom, but it is, without a doubt, one that leads her to use a condom if she should sleep with another man.

Chapter 7

Suggestions for Prevention

We cannot implement effective prevention measures unless we are familiar with the sexual culture in which we are going to work. Even when we think we are familiar with it, our points of reference may be very different from those of the target population. In the case of prisons, two parallel cultures exist that interact with each other: the culture of the prison staff and that of the inmates. Because each culture assigns a different meaning to common terms, communications may sometimes resemble a "dialogue between the deaf." To a prison officer, for example, a homosexual is a man who has sex with other men, regardless of what he does in bed. For an inmate, a man who has sex with women or with men, is not considered to have renounced heterosexuality, provided that he practices penetration. When a prison official gives a workshop that covers the subject of homosexuality, participants may understand very different things. The Health Ministry's AIDS-prevention campaign, with its emphasis on monogamy or fidelity for heterosexuals and condom use for homosexuals (and indifference toward bisexuals), means that inmates get the message the wrong way around: they are faithful to their women and do not use a condom with them, but they do use condoms with men. "I pay a lot of attention to what Dr. Herrera says [director of the Department for the Control of AIDS]," says Pico de Lora. "I'm totally faithful to my wife, and I use a condom with men. That's what the old broad always says the few times she's been here." This behavior has a certain logic, though it is counterproductive in the prevention of HIV infection. We have seen that the word "bisexual" does not have the same meaning for prison inmates as it does for prison staff. For inmates, a bisexual is a man who engages in active and passive anal penetration. "Bisexuals are the ones most at risk, because they give their ass," explains Toro. "In the case of *cacheros*, we don't do it. When the nurse asks me if I'm bisexual, I say, 'No way!' So, she tells me that I won't have any problem with infection."

Prevention cannot be enforced. The Health Ministry has promoted AIDS testing among inmates as a means of prevention. In theory, all inmates should take the test. But in practice, the ministry does not have the budget to cover the cost of tests, and figures from the Department for the Control of AIDS show that only 10 percent of the prison population has been tested. Even if it were possible to test all inmates, the fact that HIV antibodies may take weeks, months, or even a year to develop undermines the effectiveness of the testing process: hundreds of already-infected convicts may enter prison without showing signs of antibodies. To be effective, AIDS testing must be carried out frequently, not just annually. But this would further increase costs.

When we are not aware of the reality of a situation, campaigns can be misdirected. For example, confronted with the growth of HIV infection among heterosexual women, the Department for AIDS Control has launched an information campaign directed at women that promotes condom use. However, in a *machista* society, the housewife who is faithful to her husband will be unable to introduce condom use unless her spouse agrees. Husbands, however, are a much more difficult group to reach than housewives, and few efforts are being made to contact them. For this reason, prevention is ineffective. The same happens in prisons. Distributing condoms to transvestites and obvious homosexuals is an easier task because they are more visible. But it is the *cacheros* and the clients who decide whether or not a condom is used. These hard-to-access groups should also be the targets of prevention campaigns. "It's very difficult for a transvestite to make her partner use a condom," Lulu tells us. "When I tell my guy that it would be better to use one, he asks me if I'm sleeping with other men. 'No way!' I tell him, all serious, 'Don't you know how much I love you?' I ask indignantly. I play the fool, because if he ever finds out that I get the drugs he takes by whoring, he'd kill me."

I hope that this book has shown that the separation of homosexuals from the rest of the prison inmates is a fantasy. Some prisons in

Central America believe that placing homosexuals in separate cells is one way to prevent sexual relations. However, as we have seen, the ones the prison authorities regard as homosexuals are generally transvestites and very effeminate men. The inmates agree that the latter are the only real homosexuals, even though in practice they may also be homosexuals themselves: nearly 70 percent of prison inmates have sex with each other. "Look," says Pico de Lora, "if you want to separate the gays from the rest, you'd have to build a new prison and only leave the old guys that nobody wants to touch. Prison is one great gay bar and if someone doesn't join in, it's because he can't get it up," he concludes with a smile.

The approach taken by the Costa Rican Ministry of Justice is, in fact, the best alternative: prevention through education and the participation of the target population.

Given the high level of sexual activity in prison and its complexity, the nongovernmental organization ILPES agreed to implement an AIDS prevention program in the penitentiaries, in close collaboration with the Ministry of Justice. In Costa Rica, both this ministry and the General Directorate of Social Adaptation, which is in charge of prisons, have pursued a very intelligent and practical policy with respect to AIDS prevention. Instead of forcing inmates to undergo mandatory AIDS testing, or persecuting those who are sexually active, they have placed themselves in the vanguard of Latin America as far as education is concerned. Their approach has been to stop the epidemic with the participation of the inmates themselves in efforts to prevent the spread of HIV infection and related factors, such as drug consumption and violence. This plan rejected, from the outset, the Health Ministry's more repressive policy of trying to stop the spread of the disease through mandatory AIDS testing and the persecution of homosexuality.[1]

Despite the fact that prison medical facilities are controlled by the Ministry of Health, many education programs are under the jurisdiction of the Justice Ministry. This has made it possible to implement two parallel initiatives in the country's penitentiaries: the Justice Ministry's program, which may be termed holistic, and the Health Ministry's program, which follows the biomedical model of prevention.

There is no single biomedical model, but many versions. However, they share the following characteristics:

1. Information is considered the main tool to combat an epidemic. If people are well informed about how an infectious agent is transmitted and prevented, they will adopt the necessary hygiene measures to control it.
2. Information should be presented in clear, scientific language and conveyed in an authoritative manner to prevent misinterpretation or confusion among the target population.
3. Epidemics are fought by health experts (mainly doctors) who have received appropriate training to combat them. It is assumed that these experts are respected in the community and that their advice is accepted and followed.
4. The main actor in prevention efforts is the state, since one of its functions is to safeguard public health.

DRAWBACKS

While these principles are almost unquestionable, they are not altogether effective:

1. Many studies question the fundamental role of information as the sole vehicle of prevention. In epidemics such as AIDS, people are well aware how the disease is transmitted but do not automatically apply this knowledge in practice. A number of attitudes and emotions come into play, so that knowledge is not the fundamental issue. Condom use, as we have seen, is influenced by alcohol or drug consumption, for example. If people are intoxicated, they may not use a condom, no matter how much they may know about prevention.[2]
2. People are not blank screens that can be filled with information. Attitudes determine whether messages are received or repressed. Boring scientific messages are generally rejected by target populations. Unless creativity is used to make people pay attention to the message, there is a degree of saturation.[3]
3. Health experts tend to belong to the middle and upper social classes. This reduces their impact among the lower classes, who tend to mistrust their motives.

4. In third world countries, the state is generally a bureaucratic body with little flexibility and credibility, and seldom commands the people's trust.

THE HOLISTIC MODEL

This model has many variations and several origins. In the United States, it is associated with the birth of alternative medicine during the 1960s and studies on the role of the emotions in health. Although a branch of early psychiatry studied the connection between personality and disease, the holistic boom began with work in fields such as biofeedback, the role of emotional attitudes in curing cancer, and studies on nutrition, diet, and health. These different currents are based on a common premise, which is that individuals can produce and cure diseases, and that these are the result of imbalances in their lives. According to this view, prevention and cure depend on the individual, and Western medicine, with its emphasis on curing through surgery and synthetic medicines, is mistrusted.

For a prevention model to be considered holistic—in other words, one that takes account of body and mind—it must fulfill some of the following basic criteria:

1. Emotions play as important a role as reason. If a person is not emotionally convinced of the need to adopt prevention practices for his or her own good, or does not have help in doing so, he or she will not be able to make the necessary changes.
2. Prevention cannot be undertaken in an authoritative manner. The individual concerned must be a participant in his or her own well-being. This means that the target population must be actively involved in the prevention campaign, not a mere passive spectator.
3. For people to feel that a problem concerns them, it is important for them to see others like themselves, with their resources and ideology, becoming involved in the struggle. "Experts" tend to deny power to individuals by portraying themselves as the ones with all the answers.

4. The community and the individual are the main vehicles of prevention. It is at this level that we find awareness of local conditions and the main obstacles.

We can say that the Ministry of Justice has adopted a holistic approach to AIDS prevention, while the Health Ministry has adopted a biomedical one. The explanation for these ideological differences between the two ministries would require a separate book. However, we can say that officials of the Justice Ministry—lawyers, psychologists, social workers, and criminologists—have training that is closer to the humanist principles of the social sciences. Moreover, during the 1970s, Costa Rica's penitentiary system underwent major reform and shifted its focus toward the education and social reintegration of prisoners. This spirit remains alive today, and justice officials feel proud of the fact that they do not promote punitive policies toward offenders. The Health Ministry, on the contrary, adopts a more conservative approach. With a few exceptions, the doctors who work in the prison system follow the traditional model of prevention through information alone.

The holistic approach to AIDS prevention in prison is based on the following principles:

Respect for Inmates' Relationships

It is assumed that homosexuality is common in prisons and all types of couples or sexual orientations are welcomed and encouraged to participate in the program.

Participatory Methodology

The methodology used to conduct the sessions is participatory. In other words, it is a process in which members of a group participate on an equal footing. To this end, a horizontal system of communication is established through games, exercises, role playing, meditation, videos, and other mechanisms. In this participatory process, an inmate's freedom to be and do is a priority. So too is his spontaneous, active, creative, and reflexive expression, so that he can contribute to individual and collective decisions concerning matters related to AIDS and his own lifestyle.

Empowerment

Workshops are initiated by facilitators trained by ILPES and the Justice Ministry, but training is also given to prison leaders themselves so that they can replicate the workshops and assume responsibility for prevention efforts.

Administrative Independence

Although the workshops are endorsed by the Justice Ministry, they are autonomous. This gives the prisoners confidence that whatever they say will not be used against them.

The workshops consist of eight sessions and cover the following subjects.

The Rules of the Game

In the first session, the inmates establish, by consensus, the conditions under which they wish to participate. In addition, they evaluate different aspects of prison life that tend to increase the risk of HIV infection through sexual transmission.

AIDS and Safer Sex

In this session, inmates familiarize themselves with the key aspects of the disease: terminology, means of transmission, prevention, safer sex, and the AIDS test.

Overcoming Anger

During this session, participants analyze the advantages and disadvantages of uncontrolled anger, and explore how to identify and control it and the effect that a lack of emotional self-expression may produce in the individual.

Sexuality

The idea is to create gender awareness (what it is, how it is developed, differences between masculine and feminine) and in addition, an attempt is made to reduce hostility toward people who do not fit in with established sexual stereotypes.

Self-Esteem

In this session, participants explore critical factors that affect the development of self-esteem, specifically incarceration and the marginal status of prison inmates.

Holistic Health

This session tries to create awareness of the connection between body and mind, to help inmates understand how they can take charge of their own health.

Alcoholism and Drug Dependence

Available information is shared: origin, detection, consequences, and therapy alternatives, among others. Denial of the problem is also discussed as well as how prison can contribute to make inmates more vulnerable to addiction.

Power

This session considers the inmates' situation and the power they can develop in a prison environment through solidarity, working together, the care of infected inmates and their contribution to prevention among their companions.

To date, this model has been used with more than 1,000 prison inmates (in groups of ten to fifteen participants), or approximately 20 percent of the prison population. Workshops have been given at prisons throughout the country, including the following: La Reforma, San José (San Sebastián), Puntarenas (El Roble), Cartago, and Heredia. The prisons of Limón and Guanacaste were included in the process during the second half of 1993.

In analyzing the information, it should be noted that each participant was given a pretest at the start of the first session and a posttest at the end of the last session. The questionnaire, which was completed individually by each participant, was the same at the beginning and at the end, and was designed around a series of questions that attempt to measure the impact of the various themes discussed at the workshop sessions. According to the results of the evaluation, the holistic workshops are more effective than the biomedical ones: they provide greater knowledge about AIDS and prevention, reduce the tendency to reject condoms, and increase condom use. Moreover, they enhance the participants' self-esteem and sexual communication.[4] However, although the results are good, they are not sufficiently effective to halt the epidemic, since more than 60 percent of inmates still do not always use condoms. Despite the capacity of the prison staff, more radical measures may be necessary.

SEXUAL EDUCATION

During the initial diagnostic phase, each new inmate should be given a sexual education workshop. We have seen how an individual who has been convicted and sentenced undergoes a short period of observation prior to entering the cells. This preparation time, however, does not include information about the sexual culture the inmate will encounter in jail. Many new inmates arrive and witness homosexual scenes for which nobody prepared them. Others do not know how to avoid rape. Many are traumatized within twenty-four hours of their arrival. Whether we like it or not, it is necessary to explain the rules of the game in this culture to all new inmates.

Sexual education should include everyone in the prison. One of the positive aspects of the Justice Ministry's campaign has been precisely to improve awareness of sexual culture and AIDS among all prison staff, from the policeman at the prison gate, to the prison officers, to the prison director. Reducing disinformation about the dangers of infection and homophobia has made it possible to create a climate of universal support for the prevention programs. Guards who once searched inmates for condoms, supposedly to prevent homosexuality, no longer do so. Prison officers who once punished those discovered in the act of anal sex, have become more tolerant.

However, it is necessary to ensure that this more liberal attitude is reflected on paper, that it becomes official.

ACCEPTING THE LESSER EVIL

If we hope to do prevention work within a sexual culture, we must respect that culture's own leaders and institutions. In our case, this means suspending moral judgments and accepting what exists.

One example of this has to do with danger. For a middle-class, noncriminal population, any risk should be avoided. But for prison inmates, danger is part of life: they have risked danger to rob, kill, swindle, deal drugs, and commit the crimes for which they are in jail. It is only to be expected that risk is present in their relationships. We have seen how couples are formed and how they live immersed in situations of risk: rape, death threats, intimidation, prostitution, and drugs. HIV infection is simply one more risk among the many that exist in prison—and perhaps not the worst or the most immediate. With people who live amid so much danger, possibly one form of prevention may be to reduce the risk, rather than try to eradicate it completely. Inmates, for example, are willing to use a condom in their furtive relationships, or with prostitutes, but not in their intimate relationships. In the latter, the condom is a threat. Making promises that generate a certain risk may be more important to them than we think. Nevertheless, the *cachero* and the transvestite or the *güila* who swear to be faithful to each other are practicing prevention, though not necessarily in the most effective manner. Challenging this decision as "ineffective" is perhaps not the best response. Perhaps we shall have to content ourselves with promoting 70 percent rather than 100 percent effectiveness. This may not be easy to accept for officials and NGOs involved in prevention work. However, failure to consider this option may be even more counterproductive if a target population feels that a campaign deprives them of their pleasures and their promises. By striving for the optimum, we may lose the possible minimum.

RECOGNITION OF HOMOSEXUAL COUPLES

The connection between love, trust, and fidelity as forms of prevention lead many to take unnecessary risks. The hostility of some prison officers toward homosexual relationships accentuates this problem. If inmates could have support in their relationships, and even official recognition that would allow them certain benefits such as conjugal visits, privacy, medical tests, and counseling for their particular problems, then prevention would be more effective. For example, if a couple opted for fidelity as a means of prevention and were officially registered as a couple in order to receive this type of support, they could be offered optional AIDS testing, condoms, privacy, and counseling. Instead of punishing them and separating them, as sometimes happens, this official recognition would serve to promote safe sex. Instead of spending hundreds of thousands of colones on blood tests for the entire prison population to detect HIV antibodies, which is the Health Ministry's somewhat ineffective policy, the test would be available to those who need it.

As Penélope tells us, "We're not idiots, we know we can get infected. What happens is that they won't leave us in peace with our husbands. Any officer can separate us if he feels like it or if we have an argument, but who doesn't fight in this world? So then they separate us and instead of being alone with your man, you end up being raped by ten guys in another block."

Recognition of couples in jail will not be an easy step, even for one of the most progressive government ministries on the continent. However, it will be necessary to take it.

ASSISTANCE IN DETOXIFICATION

No prevention campaign can isolate itself from other problems that affect prison inmates. Drug consumption is a factor related to unsafe sex. If we do not implement a parallel campaign to prevent intoxication, we will not succeed in halting the spread of the HIV virus. Once again, it is a matter of choosing the lesser evil. It is very difficult to completely eradicate drug use in prisons. Since we must reluctantly accept this evil, our objective should be to persuade inmates to use condoms, even when they use drugs. Disposable hypodermic needles should be supplied to whoever needs them, in the same way as they are made available to intravenous drug users on the streets. Those who consume marijuana and crack should be taught techniques to avoid being caught without condoms in the case of having sexual relations. Prevention should begin before drugs are consumed. It is at this time that the inmates can think clearly. Some inmates who do not take drugs can be trained to supply condoms to their intoxicated colleagues. Others can take turns at looking after them.

PREVENTION OF VIOLENCE

We have seen how group rapes are anything but loving sexual encounters. That means that all messages urging people to use condoms as a way of taking care of their partners are useless under these circumstances. Inmates also use sex as a form of punishment. A prevention campaign should include workshops on violence with a view to reducing such attacks. ILPES has developed a behavioral workshop to control violence, known as TICO (Intensive Control Workshop), which has produced very good results. However, it is necessary to offer alternatives to inmates who have been raped, such as antiproteasic drugs to counteract possible infection, and emotional support. An information campaign should include the issue of rape as a possible source of infection, to ensure that all inmates, including the rapists, are made aware of the dangers.

PLAYING WITH FREE TIME

When a sentence is long, it seems eternal. This is especially true if the prison offers no education or work activities. Part of the attraction of intoxication is precisely to shorten time: to make the days go faster. All prevention campaigns should take account of the need to offer an alternative to drugs. In fact, one of the tasks facing ILPES and the Justice Ministry has been to think up ingenious alternatives to drugs, such as workshops based on the concept of magical realism and cooperatives which the inmates find so exciting that they have less need for drugs.

One successful experience has been the Experimental Workshop on Addictions. Its main objective is to show inmates the reasons why they need drugs and suggest alternative ways of "getting high" without them. The program does not assume that all participants will stop taking drugs. Nor does it moralize about drug use. Instead, the workshop uses a wide range of approaches, from music to magic rituals, such as painting blue unicorns. The inmates enter into a "magical" world in which mystical experiences are stimulated, either to stretch time or make it shorter. The idea is to give inmates different tools so that they themselves can play with time without the need for drugs. Considerable understanding has been required from the prison officers for them to accept rhythmic dancing sessions, aerobics, weight training, mural painting, meditation, Gregorian chant, Caribbean music, and other unusual activities in the prisons. Some complain that the inmates enjoy too many entertainments that they do not deserve. However, this daring program has given good results. Many prisoners enjoy the activities so much that they do without a marijuana joint or a dose of crack.

MICROENTERPRISES

Parallel to these workshops, considerable imagination has been used to train inmates in how to establish small businesses that are "addictive." When the Justice Ministry and ILPES introduced computer classes as a form of AIDS prevention, few understood the connection. However, the introduction of computers was well considered. "Which educational tool has color, light, and sound and at the same time creates an addiction similar to a drug trip?" This was the question we asked ourselves before coming up with the idea. In fact, the computer makes time fly just as fast as any hit from marijuana or crack. Inmates who participate in workshops to obtain a certificate in computer studies spend hours sitting in front of a computer screen and they have set up creative businesses such as their own newspaper, desktop publishing, and other services. Other creative ideas have been ecological projects such as breeding iguanas and *tepezcuintles* (*agouti paca,* small Central American mammals), hydroponics (growing plants and vegetables in water), and art exhibitions. However, these programs reach only a small number of inmates, so their impact is still limited.

To conclude, it is important to recognize that Costa Rica's Ministry of Justice and ILPES have been leaders in the field of AIDS prevention in prisons. However, they are committed to continue taking new risks. Just as sexual relations between inmates involve risk, so it is also necessary to take risks in the prevention of AIDS.

Epilogue

Eight years have passed since I first went into the prisons. In that time, I could have committed a murder and served my sentence. It is obviously very different to go to prison every day and be able to leave at five in the afternoon. Nevertheless, it is never easy to be in there, even when you know that at the end of the day you can go home and forget, at least for a while, the suffering you have witnessed. It is also impossible not to become fond of the inmates, including those who have committed horrible crimes. Even the venomous Clitoris became my friend. The poor thing was very disappointed when I told her that she would not be the main star of my study, though I promised her that if I ever wrote a book about transvestites in jail, she would be the first to feature in it. With some resignation, she later told me about her many adventures in her cell. She could not decide between Burro and Calza de Muela, two of her suitors. On several occasions I tried to encourage her to choose Burro, because I felt that he was her best bet—he still had all his teeth. However, a week later, Clitoris would be back with Calza de Muela, because, she said, "What good are teeth to me, anyway?" She was eventually released, only to be murdered a few weeks later in Panama. They say she was found with her throat cut, in a pool of blood.

On other occasions I listened to Pedro's stories. He had killed three people, including a transvestite in Heredia prison. I remember hearing his excuse—that his victim had asked for it—as I noticed, out of the corner of my eye, that the guards had locked the cell we were in. What would happen if he turned violent? Would I end up as mincemeat? I wondered. But he had no feelings of violence toward me. His anger had been aroused by the infidelity, the betrayal of the transvestite. While Pedro proudly told me how he had stabbed his victim with a knife and how he had then cleaned up the "mess" because he didn't like "filth," I thought of the poor transvestite who had fallen in love with Pedro. "But Pedro, don't you think it's a bit crazy to have killed him because he went with another man?" I couldn't help asking him. "He knew I was very jealous and he loved me to spy on him," was his reply.

One day I had to comfort Toro because Angelita no longer went to visit him. She had been released from prison and it was rumored that she prostituted herself on the street. "No, no, Toro. How can you think that she'll betray you with someone else, when she loves you so much?" I said hypocritically, to alleviate his suffering. "She's a transvestite and you know how they flirt in the street," he said, weeping. "I know many transvestites who are very decent housewives, faithful to their husbands, who go to church and are Christians," I said. "Well, that's because the bitches are fucking the priest," was his reply. I remained silent because the truth was, I had seen Angelita whoring the night before on a corner in the Clinica Biblica (a well-known haunt of transvestite prostitutes).

I cannot deny that I also had my suitors. Once a handsome young man sent me a love poem. It said I was the ideal man for him, that he found me extremely attractive and that I was the main character of his erotic fantasies. Although it would never occur to me to have a relationship that was unprofessional, I cannot deny that my ego felt somewhat inflated. When I told my work colleague that I was still considered attractive, my illusions were quickly shattered. "But don't you know that this guy likes to strangle old foxes?" he said.

I do not believe that the criminal mind exists. Rather, I believe that there are people with less control over their instincts. As Pico de Lora, my guide during all these years, says, "Criminality is latent in all of us." Any one of us, given the right circumstances, can fall into it. We are susceptible to good and evil; if you do not believe me, read about what happened to the Jews in the Holocaust. I cannot stop thinking that those who end up in jail are, in their great majority, the poor. I know many respected businessmen who have swindled the government. Others have made fortunes from contra-band. Every day, some bureaucrat steals the people's money and very few are tried and punished. The big drug dealers generally do not end up behind bars. Are these not the ones who really deserve to rot in jail? On the other hand, some poor devil who has stolen a pig or a color television is locked up. As Toro says, in this country, the law is to punish the poor. "The rich can even kill and a few days later, they're drinking martinis in the Country Club, while they discuss Aristotle with their buddies," he concludes.

But I am not here to write a book about the judicial system. I am here to describe a sexual culture, though Pico de Lora (and many orthodox historians) may doubt that sex is part of culture. Some will believe that sexuality is an instinct like hunger and that we are programmed to respond to the call of reproduction (the only normal form of sexuality, according to them). If I have learned anything from this study, it is that sexuality is more elastic than we would like to admit. We are a product of our culture. This does not mean that we cannot make changes and break out of the mold, but these changes and "rebellions" are responses to what has been handed to us. Few people invent something new. There is a limit to what we can do with our bodies and minds. For this reason, I do not think our sexual orientation is determined by hormones, genes, or differences in the hypothalamus. If that were true, *cacheros* would not exist.

I do not believe that I know any more about sexuality than the inmates. Some "experts" have told me that inmates are really homosexuals, like any gay, who simply do not dare to come out of the closet. A gay journalist told me bluntly: "If they could live their sexuality openly, without fearing rejection, they'd all be gay." I do not believe that. I have learned to differentiate between gay culture or homosexual culture and the culture established by other minorities such as prisoners, sailors, prostitutes, policemen, and others with extensive experience of sex with men. Inmates are not homosexuals in the broadest sense of the term: the majority do not feel attracted to other men; they like women and do not share a background of having "felt different," which is common among homosexuals (though not universal). Gays have no right to claim as their own minorities who do not wish to have anything to do with them, and have no desire to be represented by their "leaders." Pico de Lora himself confirms this: "One evening this queen who's the head of some gays' organization calling itself the Pinks or the Triangulars came out speaking on behalf of all men who have sex with men. Who wants to be represented by some effeminate faggot? If I felt I was a part of that group I'd rather slash my wrists."

With regard to the relations I have described, I have learned much about human sexuality. The prisoners' need to establish asymmetrical relationships also has its logic. In a patriarchal society such as ours, gender differences are so great that heterosexuals have no need to add more differences to the ones they already have: men and women are beings who are socialized differently. But in the case of relations between men, both have been raised in a similar way. To maintain the chemistry of attraction, it is necessary for some to play a different role from the others. According to Pico de Lora, "People are attracted to something different, to what they don't have." If his argument is correct, prison culture stimulates this differentiation to maintain the interest of some in others. Perhaps one of the most basic motives for sexual attraction is the desire to possess what one does not have; perhaps not. The *cacheros* will seek the most feminine part in the transvestite and vice versa, and the older man will be drawn to the youth of the *güila*. The foxes will look for qualities other than youth or femininity.

Prison culture is not much different from the culture of other sexual minorities. When Pico de Lora asked me, the day we met, why I was interested in writing this book, I did not have an answer. Now perhaps I have a better idea. Minorities have many things in common. One of these is that we are confined by prisons, real or imaginary: our space is limited; there are places which we cannot enter; our bodies have been colonized and our differences have been silenced. "Yes, Pico de Lora, though you may not believe me, I know what it's like to live in a prison too," I can now tell him. "But you've got money, you can leave this place and rub shoulders with the people who've got all the dough. How can you compare yourself with me?" was his reply. "But Pico de Lora, tell me the truth, don't lie to me, don't try to please me, don't oil the wheels. Am I the same as the guards, the ministers, the prison officials, the priests, the lawyers?" I asked without knowing the answer. "No, you're crazy. You come in here, where everyone wants to get out, you eat the same shit we do, you bring workshops and entertainments, you've cried with us, you haven't looked to see what you can take or get out of this, you're crazy," was his reply. "Thank you, Pico de Lora. That's the best thing I've heard in my whole life. It's time to go and write this book." My guide escorted me to the fence that separates the two worlds and gave me a hug. I feel like Orpheus, who descended into Hell in search of something lost, trying not to look back this time.

Notes

Chapter 1

1. Schifter, Jacobo and Madrigal, Johnny. *Hombres que aman hombres*, ILEP-SIDA, San José, Costa Rica, 1992.

2. Madrigal, Johnny. *Impacto de la prevención del sida en privados de libertad costarricenses*, ILPES, San José, Costa Rica, 1993, p. 1.

3. The transvestites' real names, like those of the rest of the inmates, have been changed. However, I have given the former feminine names, since they prefer to use them.

4. Madrigal, Johnny. *Impacto de la prevención del sida en privados de libertad costarricenses*, ILPES, San José, Costa Rica, 1993, p. 18.

5. Hart, G. *Sexual maladjustment and disease: An introduction to modern venerology.* Nelson-Hall, Chicago, 1973.

6. Havelock, Ellis, quoted in Fishman, Joseph F. *Sex practices of prisoners,* Padell Book Co., USA, 1951, p. 79.

7. Fishman, Joseph F. *Sex practices of prisoners*, Padell Book Co., USA, 1951, p. 81.

8. Madrigal, Johnny. *Impacto de la prevención del sida en privados de libertad costarricenses*, ILPES, San José, Costa Rica, 1993, p. 18.

9. Schifter and Madrigal, *Hombres que aman hombres*, p. 184.

10. Madrigal, Johnny. *Impacto de la prevención del sida en privados de libertad costarricenses*, ILPES, San José, Costa Rica, 1993, p. 14.

Chapter 4

1. Foucault, Michel. *La historia de la sexualidad.* 1/-18th ed Siglo XXI, Mexico City, 1991.

2. Foucault, Michel. *The history of sexuality, Volume 1: An introduction,* trans. Robert Hurley, Vintage, New York, 1980, p. 96.

Chapter 5

1. Schifter, Jacobo and Madrigal, Johnny. *Hombres que aman hombres*, ILEP-SIDA, San José, Costa Rica, 1992, p. 190.

Chapter 6

1. Schifter, Jacobo and Madrigal, Johnny. *Hombres que aman hombres,* ILEP-SIDA, San José, Costa Rica, 1992.

2. Ibid.

3. Stall, R., McKusick, L., Coates, W.J., and Ostrow, D. "Alcohol and drug use during sexual activity and compliance with safe sex guidelines for AIDS: The AIDS behavioral research project," *Health Education Quarterly,* Winter 1986, 13(4):359-371.

4. Bye, L. *A Report on: Designing an effective AIDS prevention campaign strategy for San Francisco: Results for the fourth probability sample of an urban gay male community.* Report prepared by Communications Technology for The San Francisco AIDS Foundation, 1987.

5. Connell, R.W., Crawford, J., and Kippax, S. *Social aspects of the prevention of AIDS: Report 1. "Methods and sample." Report 2. "Information about AIDS: The accuracy of knowledge possessed by gay and bisexual men,"* Australia, Macquarie University, 1988.

6. Baumann, L. and Siegel, K. "Misperception among gay men of the risk of AIDS associated with their sexual behavior." *Journal of Applied Social Psychology,* 1987, 17(3):329-350.

7. Prieur, A. "Gay men: Reasons for continued practice of unsafe sex." Presented at the First International Symposium on Information and Education on AIDS, Ixtapa, Mexico, 1988.

8. Bye, L. *Designing an effective AIDS prevention campaign strategy for San Francisco: Results for the fourth probability sample of an urban gay male community.* Report prepared by Communications Technology for The San Francisco AIDS Foundation, 1985.

9. Connell, R.W., Crawford, J., and Kippax, S. *Social aspects of the prevention of AIDS: Report 1. "Methods and sample." Report 2. "Information about AIDS: The accuracy of knowledge possessed by gay and bisexual men,"* Australia, Marquarie University, 1988.

10. Schifter, Jacobo and Madrigal, Johnny, *Hombres que aman hombres.* ILEP-SIDA, San José, Costa Rica, 1992.

11. Ibid.

Chapter 7

1. For an analysis of the Costa Rican Health Ministry's repressive campaign we recommend our book, Schifter, Jacobo, *La formación de una contracultura: Homosexualismo y sida en Costa Rica*, Editorial Guayacán, San José, Costa Rica, 1989.

2. Madrigal, Johnny. *Primera encuesta nacional sobre sida: Informe de resultados.* (First national survey on AIDS: Report on the results.) Johnny Madrigal Pana, Jacobo Schifter Sikora, Costa Rican Demographic Association, San José, Costa Rica, ADC, 1990.

3. Abrahams Vargas, Maritza. *Impacto de los mensajes sobre salud reproductiva transmitidos por radio y televisión en los adolescentes de los centros educativos Metodista y José Joaquín Vargas Calvo.* (Impact of reproductive health messages broadcast on radio and television among adolescents at the Methodist and José Joaquín Vargas Calvo high schools.) Thesis submitted to obtain a master's degree in nursing. University of Costa Rica, San José, Costa Rica, 1993.

4. Madrigal, Johnny. *Impacto de la prevención del sida en privados de libertad costarricenses.* ILPES, San José, Costa Rica, 1993, p. 1.

Index

Page numbers followed by the letter "t" indicate tables.

Accidental, sex with transvestite, 27
Administrative independence, 95
Admission, prison, 3-7
AIDS, 14. *See also* Unsafe sex
   prevention, 101
     biomedical model, 91-93
     holistic model, 93-97
   and rape, 73
   and safer sex, 95
AIDS testing, *ix,* 90, 95
AIDS-prevention workshops
   and the Health Ministry, 89
   and ILPES, *ix,* 1-2
   inmate participation in, 10, 14, 83,
     85-86
Alcohol, 96
   and unsafe sex, 81-83
Anal sex, 2
   and condom use, 83-87, 85t
   for money, 67
Anger, 95
Animal breeding, and AIDS
     prevention, 101
Art exhibitions, and AIDS
     prevention, 101
Attacks, in prison. *See* Rape

Baumann, L., 82
Beauty pageants, transvestite, 10
Biomedical prevention model, 91-92
   drawbacks to, 92-93
Bisexuals, 12, 54, 89-90
Blacklisted, 59

Boredom, with penetration only, 32
Bye, L., 82, 83

Cacherismo, 15, 18, 27, 57, 63
Cacheros, 2, 11, 14, 15
   as *coles,* 18
   güilas becoming, 51
   and kids (*güilas*), 35-45
   as killers, 48-49
   and love, 33-34
   not homosexual, 13
   as penetrator, 18
   traditional, 29-31
   and transvestites, 17-29, 57
   using companion, 34
Cell, prison, 7-8
   rape in, 8-9
Center for Institutional Attention
     of San José, 3
Central Penitentiary, San José, 45
Chicha, 81, 82
Cocaine, 82
Coles, 18, 57-58, 62-63
   stealing from, and rape, 79-80
"Colonized," 60
Commitment, *güilas* and, 47-50
Competition, and prostitution, 67-68
Computer classes, and AIDS
     prevention, 101
Condoms, 83-87, 85t
   distribution of, 90
Confidential, rape, 73
Conjugal visits, 12
Connell, R. W., 82

Couples
  commitment, *güila,* 47-50
  married, 11
    de facto marriage, 33
  recognition of, 98-99
Crack, 46, 82

Danger, 98
De facto marriage, 33
Den. *See* Cell, prison
Department for the Control of AIDS,
    ix, 89, 90
Desperation, 6-7
Detoxification, 99-100
Dialect, prisoner's own, 61-62
"Dialogue between the deaf," 89
Discourse, alternative, 61. *See also*
    Cacherismo
Disease, homosexuality viewed as, 13
Dormitory, and rape, 74
Drawbacks, to prevention, 92-93
Drugs, 96
  and detoxification, 99-100
  and unsafe sex, 81-83

Ellis, Havelock, 11-12
Empowerment, 95
"Environmentalist," view of
    homosexuality, 14-15
"Essentialist," view of
    homosexuality, 14-15
Exclusivity, 46-47
Experimental Workshop on
    Addictions, 100-101

Fellatio, 51. *See also* Oral sex
"Feminizing" a man, 59
Fishman, Joseph F., 12
Forced initiation, 46. *See also* Rape
Foucault, Michel, 57
Foxes (*zorras*), 17, 32, 53-57
  prison staff as, 72
  and prostitution, 71-73

Free time, 8
  and drug use, 82-83
  preventing, 100-101

Gang rape, 28
Gender awareness, 95-96
"Genetic," homosexuality viewed
    as, 15
"Godfather," 46, 74
Gonorrhea, 12
Great Traitor, 11
Güilas (young gay men), 2, 17
  becoming *cacheros,* 51
  and *cacheros,* 35-45
  and commitment, 47-50
  and foxes, 56
  and transvestites, 56-57
Guilt, and homosexuality, 24

Health Ministry, 89, 91, 94
Her. *See* Transvestite
Holistic health, 96
Holistic prevention model, 93-97
Holistic workshops, 2, 12
Homosexual couples, 17, 33, 98-99
Homosexual Response Survey, 1
Homosexuality, in prison, 11-12
  avoiding, 29
  initiation, 19-29
  inmate view of, 14-15
  in-the-closet, 12
  and overcrowding, 10
  preventing, 12
  and prison staff, 13
  and separate cells, 91
  tolerance of, 97-98
Hostility, 98-99
Hydroponics, and AIDS prevention,
    101
Hypodermic needles (disposable),
    supplying, 99

ILPES (Latin American Institute
    for Prevention and Health
    Education), *ix*, 19, 87, 91, 100
Inactivity, prison, 8
    and drug use, 82-83
    preventing, 100-101
Infidelity, 19
Informant, and rape, 79-80
Initiation
    cachero-güila relationship, 45-47
    homosexuality, 19-29
    sexual, man with older woman, 25
Inmate. *See* Prison, inmate
Insecurity, sex for relieving, 70
"International mall," 5
In-the-closet homosexual (fox), 12
Intimacy, 84-88

Justice Ministry, 91, 94, 97, 100

Kid (young man), 11, 17
    and *cacheros*, 35-45
Killer, *cachero* as, 48-49
Kissing, 9, 10, 29

La Reforma, prison, 12, 83
Latin American Institute for
    Prevention and Health
    Education (ILPES),
    ix, 19, 87, 91, 100
Lorazepam, 82
Love, *cachero*, 33-34
Lover, prison, 24

Machista society, 15
Macho, penetrator, 29
Marijuana, 82
Married couples, inmates as, 11, 33
    recognition of, 98-99
Masculine, fox as, 55. *See also* Foxes
Masturbation, 31, 51

Microenterprises, 101
Ministry of Health, 91
Ministry of Justice, *ix-x*, 91, 94
Modern, view of homosexuality, 13
Modern homosexual, 54, 63
Money, 46
Motive, for rape, 74-75

New arrivals, prison, 4

Oppression, resisting, 61
Oral sex, 29, 31
    for money, 67
Overcrowding, prison, 7-8, 9-10.
    See also Homosexuality
    and rape, 73. *See also* Rape

Paco Rabanne, spray, 5
Participatory methodology, 94
Passive oral sex, 29, 31
Payment, for sex, 67
Pedophilia, 35-45
Penetrated
    curiosity to be, 32
    feminine, 14
    güilas, 51
Penetrator
    cachero as, 18, 29
    man as, 14
    only, boredom with, 32
Penis, 29, 31
Perreras (dog cages), 3-4
Pico de Lora ("Parrot Beak"), 5-7
Power, 57, 96-97
    and sex, 58-63
    and sexual attraction, 79
Prevention
    AIDS, 101. *See also* Prevention
        models, AIDS
    detoxification, 99-100
    of free time, 100-101
    homosexuality in prison, 12
    violence, 100

Prevention models, AIDS
  biomedical, 91-93
  holistic, 93-97
Pride of belonging, 62-63
Prieur, A., 82
Prison
  admission, 3-7
  attacks. *See* Rape
  inmates
    dialect, own, 61-62
    free time, 8
      and drug use, 82-83
      preventing, 100-101
    and homosexuality, *See*
      Homosexuality, in prison
    as married couples, 11
      de facto marriage, 33
    privacy, 8
    and rape, 8
    relationships
      recognition of, 98-99
      respect for, 94
    reoffenders, 4
    and submission, 59-60
    transvestites, 7, 8, 14, 15
    and venereal disease, 12
  overcrowding, 7-8
    and rape, 73. *See also* Rape
  store, 5
Prison staff, 13
  as foxes, 72
  power, and inmates, 59
  and prostitutes, 70
  view of homosexuals, 89, 98-99
Privacy, prisoner, 8
Prostate, 18-19
Prostitution, 65, 66t
  and foxes, 71-73
  and prison staff, 70
  and transvestites, 67-70
Pulpería (corner store), 5
"Punishment of the people," rape as,
    80

Queen, 32, 72-73

Rape, 73-80, 74t
  in cell, 8-9
  and initiation, 28
  and pedophilia, 42-44
Rats, prison, 8
Rebellion, and rape, 79
Rejection, and rape, 76
Remand section, prison, 4
Reoffending prisoners, 4
Revenge, rape as, 76-77

San Sebastián, admission prison, 3
Self-esteem, 96
Serving, 18
Sex, and power, 58-63
Sex Practices of Prisoners
    (Fishman), 12
Sexual attraction, and power, 79
Sexual culture, attempts to
    "colonize," *ix-x*
Sexual education, 97-98
Sexual initiation
  cachero-güila relationship, 45-47
  homosexuality, 19-29
  man with older woman, 25
  and transvestites, 27
Sexual practice, 14, 29-33
Sexual satisfaction, 26
Sexuality, 95-96
She. *See* Transvestite
Slashing own wrist, 62
Sodomy, 11, 14, 15, 41
Stall, R., 82
Stares, avoiding inmate's, 5-6
Store, prison, 5
Stress, 10
Studies in the Psychology of Sex
    (Ellis), 12
Submission, inmate, 59-60
Syphilis, 12

Tension, sex for relieving, 70
Therapy, mandatory, 60
TICO (Intensive Control Workshop),
    100
Time, free, 8
    and drug use, 82-83
    preventing, 100-101
Toilet, and rape, 74
Traitor, fox as, 59
Transvestite, 7, 8, 15
    accidental sex with, 27
    beauty pageants, 10
    and *cacheros*, 17-29, 57
    and condoms, distribution to, 90
    and *güilas*, 56-57
    as homosexuals, 14
    penetrating, 32
    penis, not touching, 29, 31
    and prostitution, 65, 67-70
Tricks, prostitute's, 70

Unsafe sex
    and alcohol, 81-83
    and condoms, 83-84, 85t
    and drugs, 81-83
    and intimacy, 84-88

Venereal disease, 12
Violence, prevention of, 100

World Health Organization (WHO),
    ix, 1
Wrist slashing, 62

Zorras (in-the-closet homosexuals),
    2, 17, 32, 53-57
Zorrismo, 53-54

Order Your Own Copy of
This Important Book for Your Personal Library!

MACHO LOVE
Sex Behind Bars in Central America

_____ in hardbound at $29.95 (ISBN: 1-56023-965-4)

_____ in softbound at $14.95 (ISBN: 1-56023-966-2)

COST OF BOOKS _____

OUTSIDE USA/CANADA/
MEXICO: ADD 20% _____

POSTAGE & HANDLING _____
*(US: $3.00 for first book & $1.25
for each additional book)*
*Outside US: $4.75 for first book
& $1.75 for each additional book)*

SUBTOTAL _____

IN CANADA: ADD 7% GST _____

STATE TAX _____
*(NY, OH & MN residents, please
add appropriate local sales tax)*

FINAL TOTAL _____
*(If paying in Canadian funds,
convert using the current
exchange rate. UNESCO
coupons welcome.)*

☐ **BILL ME LATER:** ($5 service charge will be added)
(Bill-me option is good on US/Canada/Mexico orders only;
not good to jobbers, wholesalers, or subscription agencies.)

☐ Check here if billing address is different from
shipping address and attach purchase order and
billing address information.

Signature _____

☐ **PAYMENT ENCLOSED: $** _____

☐ **PLEASE CHARGE TO MY CREDIT CARD.**

☐ Visa   ☐ MasterCard   ☐ AmEx   ☐ Discover
☐ Diner's Club

Account # _____

Exp. Date _____

Signature _____

Prices in US dollars and subject to change without notice.

NAME _____

INSTITUTION _____

ADDRESS _____

CITY _____

STATE/ZIP _____

COUNTRY _____ COUNTY (NY residents only) _____

TEL _____ FAX _____

E-MAIL_____
May we use your e-mail address for confirmations and other types of information? ☐ Yes   ☐ No

Order From Your Local Bookstore or Directly From
The Haworth Press, Inc.
10 Alice Street, Binghamton, New York 13904-1580 • USA
TELEPHONE: 1-800-HAWORTH (1-800-429-6784) / Outside US/Canada: (607) 722-5857
FAX: 1-800-895-0582 / Outside US/Canada: (607) 772-6362
E-mail: getinfo@haworthpressinc.com
PLEASE PHOTOCOPY THIS FORM FOR YOUR PERSONAL USE.

BOF96

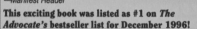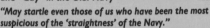